COOKING
FOR A
CROWD

FAVORITE RECIPES®
OF HOME ECONOMICS
TEACHERS

Great American Opportunities, Inc./Favorite Recipes Press

President: Thomas F. McDow III
Director of Marketing: Roger Conner
Marketing Services Manager: Karen Bird
Editorial Manager: Mary Jane Blount
Editors: Georgia Brazil, Mary Cummings, Jane Hinshaw,
Barbara Peeler, Mary Wilson
Typography: William Maul, Sharon Whitehurst

Home Economics Advisory Board

Favorite Recipes Press wants to recognize the following who graciously serve on our Home Economics Advisory Board:

Cover Photograph: Argo corn starch.

Copyright © 1987 by Great American Opportunities, Inc.
P. O. Box 77, Nashville, Tennessee 37202

Library of Congress Catalog Number is: 87-8449
ISBN: 0-87197-221-2

Manufactured in the United States of America

First Printing 1987

CONTENTS

KEYS TO SUCCESSFUL QUANTITY COOKING

Every cook encounters at some time occasions to cook for a crowd. These occasions are varied: family reunions, church suppers, formal receptions, bridal dinners, teen-age get-togethers, Cub Scout cook-outs, office picnics, ice cream socials or bridge luncheons. However, all should be festive and joyful for everyone—even the cook.

With the proper tools and advance planning, the cook need not be overwhelmed by the prospect of cooking for a large group. Step-by-step planning will establish a schedule so that events not only fall into place as they should, but the host or hostess will be relaxed enough to enjoy the occasion while making it look easy.

Planning a party around a theme or holiday can provide the framework for decision-making. After determining the type of party and its location, selecting the menu is of primary importance. The guest list and the budget must also be considered. While wieners might be a popular and practical choice for the Cub Scouts, adult guests at a rehearsal dinner will expect a more elaborate menu. The family reunion or neighborhood barbecue will cater to a variety of age groups and tastes. A luau would suggest a very specific menu.

Select the main dish first. A seated dinner will allow a wide choice of entrée from *Sweet and Sour Roast* to *Swiss Steak*. But if the guests are going to be eating from small trays or plates on their laps, choose an entrée that does not require cutting with a knife, such as *Lasagna* or *Shrimp Casserole*. Main dishes served from a buffet should be able to stand on the table without losing flavor, texture or attractiveness. The *Javanese Dinner* or *Salmagundi* would be an excellent buffet choice.

The main dish is usually the most expensive menu choice. A glance at the Quantity Buying Guide on pages 89 through 91 and the basic recipes on pages 7 and 8 will suggest the amounts of various foods required for 50 servings. These amounts can be adjusted to serve larger or smaller groups, and a price check at the grocery will provide a quick estimate of main dish cost.

Select secondary dishes to complement the entrée and the theme or occasion. Again, consider the serving and seating arrangements and keep the number of courses or plates to a minimum for meals eaten on the lap. Choose fruits and vegetables which are in season for economy, taste and appeal. The *Zucchini Casserole* and *Fresh Corn Bake* take advantage of summer's fresh produce. The *Cranberry Mold* complements a winter holiday menu.

It is important not to let the menu become too complicated. The space available for cooking and serving, the availability of help, and the time schedule should be considered. It is much wiser to serve a simple, well-prepared meal using tested recipes than to attempt an elaborate menu.

Take into account the capacity of your kitchen. Select no more than two food items to heat in the oven and be sure they can be done at the same temperature. Select dishes which are prepared in a variety of ways to take advantage of all the appliances in the kitchen. Many salads, desserts and cold vegetables on the following pages can be prepared in advance and stand in the refrigerator or freezer. Casseroles such as *Holiday Turketti, Breakfast Cheese Puff* and *Seafood-Wild Rice Casserole* can be prepared a day ahead and baked at serving time. *Jambalaya* and *Chili* can be prepared on the stove top. *Microwave Gumbo* and *Microwave Cranberry Punch* can be prepared in the microwave. By using all of these methods, preparation can be spread over several days and last-minute panic can be avoided.

Don't forget that small appliances can also make serving your dinner easier. Electric warming trays will keep appetizers and buffet dishes hot until every guest has been served and assure warm second servings for seated dinners. Foods served from a chafing dish or fondue pot are good choices for parties. They are easy for the hostess and provide an ice-breaking activity for the guests. The *Spicy Cheese Dip, Pizza Fondue* or *Spicy Baked Meatballs* can be served in this way. Many one-dish meals such as *Fancy Franks* and *Crazy Stew* can be served directly from the Crock•Pot.

Make lists. Make a grocery list from the recipes selected. Check your cupboard and refrigerator for ingredients on hand. List the cookware needed to prepare each dish, noting which items need to be bought or borrowed. Do the shopping for groceries and utensils well in advance, allowing time to find unusual items. Check the yellow pages to reduce shopping trips and save time.

Make a time schedule which allows for as much advance preparation as possible. Include such duties as table setting and flower arranging. Stick to your plan and time schedule, then you will feel confident and in control at all times. You will find yourself entertaining with ease and both you and your guests will enjoy the relaxed atmosphere.

Now that your plans are completed, it is time to cook. All of the recipes in this book will yield 12 or more servings. Most vegetable, salad and main dish recipes can be multiplied as needed to serve groups larger than the recipe suggests. Seasonings, however, should be adjusted by taste rather than by doubling. Also, exercise caution when increasing many desserts and bread recipes. You should prepare several recipes of most cakes, candies and yeast breads rather than doubling the recipes. The charts on the following pages include several basic recipes to serve 50. They may be easily halved or doubled to serve 25 or 100.

Basic Recipes To Serve 50

Beef Stew

12 pounds	Beef cubes	Brown beef in shortening in large heavy skillet; drain. Place in four 10x14-inch baking pans. Combine broth, 4 cups water, onion and seasonings in bowl. Pour over beef. Bake, covered, at 350 degrees for 1 hour. Add carrots. Bake for 1 hour. Add potatoes. Bake for 30 minutes. Add peas. Bake for 30 minutes. Blend flour and 4 cups water in bowl. Stir into stew. Cook on top of stove until thickened to desired consistency, stirring constantly.
½ cup	Shortening	
8 cans	Beef broth	
4 cups	Water	
4 cups	Chopped onion	
2 tablespoons	Salt	
2 teaspoons	Thyme	
4 pounds	Carrots, chopped	
4 pounds	Potatoes, chopped	
4 10-oz. packages	Frozen peas	
1 to 1⅓ cups	Flour	
2 cups	Water	

Chili

8 pounds	Ground beef	Brown ground beef and onion in large stockpot, stirring frequently; drain. Add remaining ingredients. Bring to a boil; reduce heat. Simmer for 45 minutes, stirring constantly.
8 cups	Chopped onion	
8 8-ounce cans	Tomato sauce	
16 cans	Kidney beans	
3 cups	Water	
⅔ cup	Chili powder	
½ cup	Vinegar	
4 cloves	Garlic, chopped	
4 teaspoons	Salt	
¼ teaspoon	Pepper	

Meat Loaf

12 pounds	Ground beef	Combine first 6 ingredients and 2 cans sauce in bowl. Shape into 4 loaves. Place in two 10x14-inch baking pans. Bake at 350 degrees for 1½ hours. Mix 4 cans tomato sauce, water and ⅔ cup pan drippings in saucepan. Heat to serving temperature. Place meat loaves on serving plates. Pour sauce over top.
3 cups	Dry bread crumbs	
2 cups	Chopped onion	
6	Eggs, beaten	
2 tablespoons	Salt	
½ teaspoon	Pepper	
6 8-ounce cans	Tomato sauce	
⅔ cup	Water	

Spaghetti With Meat Sauce

8 pounds	Ground beef	Brown ground beef and onion in large stockpot, stirring frequently; drain. Add tomato sauce, tomatoes and seasonings; mix well. Simmer for 30 minutes. Serve over spaghetti. Serve with grated Parmesan cheese.
8 cups	Chopped onion	
24 8-oz. cans	Tomato sauce	
12 16-oz. cans	Tomatoes	
10 cloves	Garlic, chopped	
¼ cup	Basil and oregano	
8 pounds	Spaghetti, cooked	

Basic Recipes To Serve 50

Glorious Chicken

100 pieces (25 lb.)	Chicken	Arrange chicken in six 12x18-inch baking pans. Drizzle with butter. Bake at 400 degrees for 50 minutes, turning once. Pour mixture of remaining ingredients over chicken. Bake for 20 minutes longer.
1½ cups	Melted butter	
9 cans	Mushroom soup	
2 tablespoons	Paprika	
1 teaspoon	Pepper	

Creole Pork Chops

50 (15 lb.)	Pork chops	Brown pork chops in large skillets; drain. Arrange chops in four 10x14-inch baking pans. Sprinkle with salt and pepper to taste. Top each with slices of onion and green pepper. Combine remaining ingredients in bowl. Pour over pork chops. Bake, covered, for 1 hour or until chops are tender. Serve with rice.
8	Onions, sliced	
8	Green peppers, sliced	
10 8-oz. cans	Tomato sauce	
3 cups	Water	
1 teaspoon	Thyme	

Scalloped Potatoes

10 packages	White sauce mix	Prepare white sauce according to package directions. Mix with milk, cheese and salt in bowl. Alternate layers of potatoes, onions and sauce in 4 greased 12x18-inch baking pans. Dot with butter. Sprinkle with paprika. Bake, covered, for 2 hours and 15 minutes or until potatoes are tender.
2½ cups	Milk	
1½ cups	Parmesan cheese	
2 teaspoons	Salt	
12 pounds	Potatoes, sliced	
2 pounds	Onions, sliced	
¼ cup	Butter	
	Paprika	

Green Bean Bake

6 cans	Mushroom soup	Blend soup, milk, soy sauce, and pepper in bowl. Add beans and 3 cans onions. Spoon into two 10x14-inch baking pans. Bake at 350 degrees for 35 minutes or until bubbly; stir. Top with remaining onions. Bake for 5 minutes longer.
3 cups	Milk	
2 tablespoons	Soy sauce	
½ teaspoon	Pepper	
12 16-oz. cans	Green beans	
6 3½-oz. cans	French-fried onions	

Macaroni And Cheese

12 packages	White sauce mix	Prepare white sauce according to package directions. Sauté onions in butter in large saucepan. Stir in white sauce, water and ⅔ of the cheese. Heat until cheese is melted, stirring occasionally. Add macaroni. Pour into four 12x18-inch baking pans. Bake at 350 degrees for 30 minutes or until bubbly; stir. Top with remaining cheese and crumbs. Bake for 5 minutes longer or until cheese melts.
2 pounds	Onions, chopped	
⅔ cup	Butter	
3 cups	Water	
6 pounds	Sharp Cheddar cheese, shredded	
5 pounds	Elbow macaroni, cooked	
1½ cups	Buttered bread crumbs	

APPETIZERS
AND
SNACKS

Delicious Cheese Ball

24 oz. cream cheese, softened
1 sm. jar dried beef, chopped
1 can chopped ripe olives, drained
1 can chopped mushrooms, drained
2 bunches green onions, chopped
1 tsp. MSG
½ c. chopped nuts

Combine cream cheese, dried beef, olives, mushrooms, onions and MSG in bowl; mix well. Shape into ball. Roll in nuts to cover well; place on serving plate. Chill until serving time. Serve with crackers. Yield: 20 servings.

Linda Wright
Idabel H.S., Foreman, AR

Mock Boursin Cheese Ball

16 oz. cream cheese, softened
2 tbsp. whipping cream
1 clove of garlic, crushed
½ tsp. each caraway seed, basil,
*   dillweed*
Lemon pepper to taste

Line 2 rinsed tuna cans with plastic wrap. Combine cream cheese and next 5 ingredients in mixer bowl. Beat at medium speed for 3 minutes. Press into prepared cans. Chill, covered, for 24 hours to 2 weeks. Remove plastic wrap. Place on serving plate. Sprinkle with lemon pepper. Let stand until of room temperature. Serve with crackers. Yield: 12 servings.

Patricia Mikulecky
Bartlesville Mid.-H.S., Bartlesville, OK

Party Cheese Ball

16 oz. cream cheese, softened
4 oz. blue cheese, crumbled
4 oz. sharp Cheddar cheese, shredded
¼ c. finely chopped onion
1 tbsp. Worcestershire sauce
Sunflower seed

Combine cheeses in mixer bowl. Let stand at room temperature until softened. Add onion and Worcestershire sauce. Beat at low speed until blended. Beat at medium speed until fluffy, scraping bowl occasionally. Chill, covered, for 8 hours or until firm. Shape into 1 large or 30 to 36 small balls. Roll in sunflower seed to coat; place on serving plate. Chill, covered, for 2 hours or until firm. Serve with assorted crackers. Yield: 30 servings.

Bobbie D. Smith
Waynoka H.S., Waynoka, OK

Pineapple Cheese Ball

16 oz. cream cheese, softened
8 oz. Cheddar cheese, grated
1   12-oz. can crushed pineapple
¼ c. chopped green pepper
1 tbsp. chopped onion
¼ c. chopped pecans
1 tbsp. parsley flakes
1 tbsp. chopped pimento
2 c. chopped pecans
2 tbsp. parsley flakes

Combine cheeses, drained pineapple, green pepper, onion, ¼ cup pecans, 1 tablespoon parsley and pimento in bowl; mix well. Shape into 1 or 2 balls. Chill, wrapped in plastic wrap, for 2 hours. Roll cheese balls in mixture of 2 cups pecans and 2 tablespoons parsley, coating well. Chill, covered, for 24 hours or longer. May store in freezer for up to 3 months. Yield: 20 servings.

Ann G. Deal
Wilkes Central Sr. H.S., Wilkesboro, NC

Braunschweiger Pâté

1 lb. braunschweiger
4 oz. cream cheese, softened
1 tbsp. milk
1 tbsp. grated onion
1 tsp. sugar
1 tsp. chili powder
4 oz. cream cheese, softened
1 tbsp. milk
⅛ tsp. Tabasco sauce

Combine first 6 ingredients in mixer bowl; beat until smooth. Shape into mound on serving plate. Chill, covered, in refrigerator. Beat 4 ounces cream cheese, 1 tablespoon milk and Tabasco sauce in mixer bowl until smooth. Spread evenly over pâté. Chill until serving time. Garnish with parsley. Serve with crackers. Yield: 12 servings.

Joyce R. Daglow
Waldron Area Sch., Waldron, MI

Spicy Cheese Dip

1 lb. hot sausage
2 lb. Velveeta cheese, chopped
1 sm. can chopped green chilies, drained
1 med. onion, chopped
½ can tomatoes with green chilies
Evaporated milk

Brown sausage in skillet, stirring until crumbly; drain. Melt cheese in double boiler. Add sausage, chilies, onion and tomatoes; mix well. Add enough evaporated milk to make of desired consistency. Spoon into chafing dish. Serve warm with nacho chips. Yield: 12-18 servings.

Leslie K. Donnell
Talawanda H.S., Oxford, OH

Cocktail Pizza

½ c. mayonnaise
1 tsp. dried sweet basil
2 cloves of garlic, crushed
¼ c. lemon juice
1 sm. dried red chili pepper
16 oz. cream cheese, softened
1 med. bottle of picante sauce
1 can ripe olives, chopped
1 med. onion, chopped
1 med. green pepper, chopped
½ c. chopped celery
1   6-oz. can baby shrimp
4 oz. sliced pepperoni
1 c. shredded mozzarella cheese
1 c. shredded Cheddar cheese

Combine mayonnaise, basil, garlic, lemon juice and red chili in blender container. Process for 30 seconds. Add cream cheese. Process until smooth. Spread evenly in 14-inch pizza pan. Layer picante sauce and mixture of olives and vegetables over cream cheese mixture. Arrange shrimp and pepperoni over top. Sprinkle with cheeses. Chill, covered, for 24 hours or longer. Serve with sturdy crackers for dipping. Yield: 24 servings.

Billie L. Perrin
Lafayette Co. C-1 H.S., Higginsville, MO

Pizza Fondue

½ lb. ground beef
1 c. chopped onion
2   10-oz. cans pizza sauce
1 tbsp. cornstarch
1½ tsp. fennel seed
1½ tsp. oregano
¼ tsp. garlic powder
1 c. grated Cheddar cheese
1 c. grated mozzarella cheese

Brown ground beef with onion in electric fondue pot on High, stirring frequently; drain. Reduce temperature to Medium. Mix pizza sauce, cornstarch and seasonings in small bowl. Add to ground beef mixture. Cook until thickened, stirring constantly. Add cheeses ⅓ at a time, mixing well after each addition. Serve warm from fondue pot with cubes of garlic bread or toasted English muffin. Yield: 12 servings.
Note: May serve over toasted English muffins as luncheon meal.

Loretta Briggs
Breckenridge Comm. Sch., Wheeler, MI

Mexican Dip

1 lg. can refried beans
8 slices crisp-fried bacon, crumbled
3 avocados
1 tbsp. lemon juice
Tabasco sauce to taste
Garlic salt to taste
8 oz. sour cream
1 jar salsa or picante sauce
1 c. grated Colby cheese
1 c. grated Monterey Jack cheese
Chopped green onions
Chopped fresh tomato

Layer beans and bacon in shallow serving dish. Mash avocados with lemon juice, Tabasco sauce and garlic salt in bowl. Spread evenly over bacon. Layer remaining ingredients in order listed over avocado mixture. Serve with chips for dipping. Yield: 12-16 servings.

Sue Smith
Bartlesville H.S., Bartlesville, OK

Spinach Dip

2   10-oz. packages frozen chopped
    spinach, thawed, drained
1   8-oz. can water chestnuts, drained,
    chopped
1 c. each sour cream, yogurt
1 c. finely chopped green onions with tops
1 clove of garlic, crushed
½ tsp. each tarragon, dry mustard
1 tsp. salt
¼ tsp. pepper

Combine all ingredients in bowl; mix well. Spoon into serving bowl. Chill, covered, for 1 hour. Serve with rye crackers or bite-sized vegetables. Yield: 4½ cups.

Bobbie D. Smith
Waynoka H.S., Waynoka, OK

Vegetable Dip

2 c. mayonnaise
1 c. sour cream
1 tbsp. lemon juice
1 tbsp. salad herbs
2 tsp. each onion powder, garlic powder
2 tsp. chopped chives
2 tsp. Worcestershire sauce
½ tsp. paprika
¼ tsp. curry powder
2 tsp. salt

Combine all ingredients in bowl; mix well. Chill for 2 hours to overnight. Serve with bite-sized fresh vegetables such as carrot and celery sticks, cauliflowerets, broccoli flowerets and green pepper, cucumber, radish and zucchini slices for dipping. Yield: 12 servings.

Esther H. Nassar
Erie-Mason H.S., Toledo, OH

Fried Cheese

2 lb. mozzarella cheese
3 eggs, beaten
1 c. milk
Italian bread crumbs
Oil for deep frying

Cut cheese into 1½ x 3-inch pieces. Freeze for 2 to 3 hours. Beat eggs with milk. Dip each cheese finger into batter; roll in crumbs. Repeat process

2 times. Deep-fry in hot oil until golden brown. Drain on paper towels. Yield: 12-15 servings.
Note: May prepare in advance by coating cheese fingers as above and freezing until time to fry and serve.

Lynette Ann Gossen
Crowley H.S., Lafayette, LA

Olive-Cheese Puffs

8 oz. sharp Cheddar cheese, grated
1 stick margarine
1 c. flour
⅛ tsp. cayenne pepper
60 stuffed olives

Let cheese and margarine stand in bowl at room temperature until softened. Mix until well blended. Add flour and cayenne pepper; mix well. Chill for 2 to 3 hours. Shape into balls around olives; place on baking sheet. Bake at 450 degrees for 8 to 10 minutes or until light brown. Yield: 5 dozen.
Note: May omit olives.

Delinda McCormick
Caldwell Co. H.S., Cadez, KY

Fruit Kabobs

1   13½-oz. can pineapple chunks
¼ c. orange marmalade
1 tsp. ginger
Seedless grapes
Maraschino cherries, drained
1   11-oz. can mandarin oranges, drained

Drain pineapple, reserving juice. Blend reserved juice with marmalade and ginger in bowl. Add pineapple chunks, grapes and cherries. Marinate in refrigerator for 1 hour. Do not marinate mandarin oranges. Drain marinated fruit. Thread pineapple, grapes, cherries and mandarin oranges alternately onto long toothpicks. Insert in oranges on serving tray to make attractive edible centerpiece. Yield: 20-25 servings.
Note: Many other fruits may be used. Experiment with different combinations.

Joyce R. Daglow
Waldron Area Sch., Waldron, MI

Patsy's Cocktail Meatballs

2 lb. lean ground beef
2 tbsp. soy sauce
1 tbsp. Worcestershire sauce
2 tbsp. minced onion
2 eggs
1 c. cornflake crumbs
2 tsp. garlic powder
2 tsp. salt
¼ tsp. pepper
1 15-oz. can cranberry sauce
⅓ c. catsup
2 tbsp. brown sugar
1 8-oz. bottle of chili sauce
1 tbsp. vinegar

Combine first 9 ingredients in bowl; mix well. Shape into small balls; place in shallow baking pan. Bake at 400 degrees until brown; drain. Melt cranberry sauce in Crock•Pot or large saucepan. Add remaining ingredients; mix well. Add meatballs. Simmer for 30 minutes or longer. Yield: 8 dozen.

Barbara P. Whitten
Richlands Mid. Sch., Richlands, VA

Spicy Baked Meatballs

2 lb. ground beef
4 slices bread, crumbled
1 tsp. salt
½ tsp. pepper
⅔ c. milk
1 c. chopped green pepper
1 c. chopped onion
6 tbsp. sugar
½ c. vinegar
1 c. catsup
½ tsp. Worcestershire sauce
½ c. water

Combine ground beef, bread crumbs, salt, pepper and milk in bowl; mix well. Shape firmly into small balls; place in shallow baking pan. Combine remaining ingredients in bowl; mix well. Pour over meatballs. Bake, uncovered, at 350 degrees for 50 minutes, stirring once. Yield: 80-100 meatballs.
Note: May shape into larger balls or small loaves for main dish servings.

Marian E. Baker
Sycamore H.S., Sycamore, IL

Swedish Meatballs

2 lb. lean ground beef
2 c. soft bread crumbs
8 oz. cream cheese, softened
¼ c. dry onion soup mix
½ tsp. salt
½ tsp. nutmeg
2 tbsp. flour
½ c. milk
1 12-oz. bottle of catsup
1 8-oz. jar currant jelly

Combine first 8 ingredients in bowl; mix well. Shape into 60 to 80 small balls. Brown lightly in large skillet, shaking skillet constantly to keep meatballs round. Cook, covered, for 20 to 25 minutes or until cooked through. Drain meatballs well. Blend catsup and jelly in skillet. Heat until bubbly. Add meatballs. Heat, covered, for several minutes until heated through.
Yield: 5 to 6 dozen.

Ann Hodgson
Dodgeland H.S., Juneau, WI

Fancy Franks

1 c. chili sauce
1 c. currant or grape jelly
3 tbsp. lemon juice
1 tbsp. mustard
2 13-oz. cans crushed pineapple, drained
4 7-oz. packages cocktail franks

Combine first 4 ingredients in large skillet. Stir in pineapple and franks. Simmer for 15 minutes. Keep warm in Crock•Pot. Serve with cocktail toothpicks. Yield: 20-25 servings.

Deon LaBathe
Hudsonville Sch., Hudsonville, MI

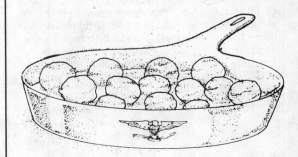

Ground Beef Tarts

½ lb. ground beef
1⅓ c. shredded Swiss cheese
⅓ c. chopped onion
1   11-oz. package pie crust mix
4 eggs, slightly beaten
1⅓ c. sour cream
1 tsp. Worcestershire sauce
1 tsp. salt

Brown ground beef in skillet, stirring until crumbly; drain. Add cheese and onion; mix well. Prepare pastry according to package directions. Roll ¹⁄₁₆ inch thick on floured surface. Cut into eighteen 4-inch circles. Fit into ungreased medium muffin cups. Spoon ground beef into pastry cups. Combine remaining ingredients in bowl; mix well. Spoon 2 tablespoons into each tart. Bake at 375 degrees for 30 minutes or until light brown. Cool in pans for 5 minutes. Yield: 18 tarts.

Bobbie D. Smith
Waynoka H.S., Waynoka, OK

Stuffed Mushrooms

12 lg. mushrooms
1 med. onion, finely chopped
½ c. chopped pepperoni
¼ c. finely chopped green pepper
1 sm. clove of garlic, minced
2 tbsp. butter
½ c. finely crushed butter crackers
3 tbsp. Parmesan cheese
1 tbsp. minced parsley
½ tsp. seasoned salt
¼ tsp. oregano
Dash of pepper
⅓ c. chicken broth

Remove mushroom stems; finely chop and reserve. Sauté onion, pepperoni, green pepper, garlic and reserved mushroom stems in butter in skillet until tender but not brown. Add remaining ingredients; mix well. Spoon into mushroom caps, rounding tops. Place in shallow baking pan. Add ¼ inch water to pan. Bake, uncovered, at 325 degrees for 25 minutes. Place on serving plate. Yield: 12 mushroom caps.

Evelyn Marvin
Fowler H.S., Fowler, CO

Miniature Broccoli Quiches

3 oz. cream cheese, softened
½ c. butter, softened
1 c. flour
5 oz. frozen chopped broccoli, thawed
1 c. shredded Swiss cheese
3 eggs
½ c. half and half
1 tsp. salt

Combine cream cheese, butter and flour in bowl; mix well. Chill until easy to handle. Shape into twenty-four 1-inch balls. Press each into greased miniature muffin cup. Drain broccoli well. Place 1 teaspoonful in each shell; top with Swiss cheese. Beat eggs with half and half and salt. Spoon 1 to 2 teaspoonfuls into each shell. Bake at 400 degrees for 25 minutes. Yield: 2 dozen.
Note: May substitute spinach, mushrooms or ham for broccoli.

Beverley C. Goodman
Smyth Co. Vo. Sch., Marion, VA

Water Chestnut Appetizers

20 slices bacon, cut in half
2 cans whole water chestnuts, drained
½ c. packed brown sugar
½ c. sugar
¾ c. catsup

Wrap 1 strip bacon around each water chestnut; place in 10x15-inch baking pan. Bake at 350 degrees for 25 minutes. Pour mixture of sugars and catsup over water chestnuts. Bake for 25 minutes longer. Yield: 40 appetizers.

Millie Morris
Richmond Hills H.S., Richmond Hill, Ga

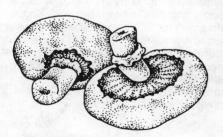

Summer Sandwich Smörgåsbord

Bobbie D. Smith
Waynoka H.S., Waynoka, OK

Cheesy Garden Sandwich

1 loaf French bread
Mayonnaise
2 c. alfalfa sprouts
Tomato slices
1 avocado, sliced
8 slices process cheese spread
8 slices crisp-fried bacon

Cut loaf into halves lengthwise. Spread cut sides with mayonnaise. Layer remaining ingredients on bottom loaf half. Top with remaining loaf half. Cut into slices. Yield: 16-20 slices.

Cajun Chicken Cushions

½ c. mayonnaise
1 tbsp. white vinegar
¼ tsp. paprika
¼ tsp. cayenne pepper
¼ tsp. salt
⅛ tsp. pepper
5 c. torn lettuce
1 c. cherry tomato halves
⅓ lg. cucumber, sliced
¼ c. chopped green pepper
1   12-oz. package frozen chicken nuggets
3 tbsp. minced parsley
2 tsp. minced garlic
2 tbsp. butter
4 whole wheat pita rounds

Combine mayonnaise, vinegar and seasonings in small bowl; mix well. Set aside. Combine lettuce, tomatoes, cucumber and green pepper in bowl; toss lightly. Set aside. Bake chicken nuggets according to package directions until almost done. Sauté parsley and garlic in butter in large skillet until light brown. Add chicken nuggets. Sauté until coated. Cut pitas into halves; open to form pockets. Place nuggets and vegetable mixture in pockets; drizzle with mayonnaise mixture. Cut each pita pocket into halves. Arrange on serving plate. Yield: 16 sandwiches.

Tempting Turkey Sandwich

1 loaf French bread
Salad dressing
¼ c. chopped walnuts
Lettuce leaves
8 slices cooked turkey
1   16-oz. can jellied cranberry sauce
8 slices process cheese spread

Cut loaf into halves lengthwise. Spread cut sides with salad dressing. Layer walnuts, lettuce and turkey on bottom half. Slice cranberry sauce ½ inch thick. Alternate slices of cranberry sauce and cheese over turkey. Top with remaining loaf half. Cut into slices. Yield: 16-20 slices.

Reuben Sandwich

⅔ c. brown mustard
2 tbsp. chili sauce
24 slices rye bread
12 slices Swiss cheese
12 slices cooked corned beef
32 oz. sauerkraut, drained
Margarine, softened

Blend mustard and chili sauce in bowl. Spread on 1 side of 12 bread slices. Layer cheese, corned beef and sauerkraut over mustard mixture. Top with remaining bread. Spread sandwiches on both sides with margarine. Grill on griddle over low heat for 10 minutes on each side or until golden and cheese begins to melt. Yield: 12 whole or 24 half sandwiches.

Surprising Salami Sandwich

8 oz. cream cheese, softened
½ c. chopped red pepper
¼ c. chopped onion
1 loaf Italian bread
12 slices salami
1 c. cucumber slices
8 oz. process cheese spread, sliced

Combine cream cheese, red pepper and onion in bowl; mix well. Cut loaf into halves lengthwise. Spread cut sides with cream cheese mixture. Layer salami, cucumber and cheese on bottom half. Top with remaining loaf half. Cut into slices. Yield: 16-20 slices.

The Stroganoffer

1 c. sour cream
¼ c. white horseradish, drained
½ tsp. salt
¼ tsp. pepper
½ lb. fresh mushrooms, sliced
1   7-inch round crusty peasant loaf
Mayonnaise
1 lb. rare roast beef, thinly sliced
16 red pepper rings
2 c. lightly packed watercress sprigs

Blend sour cream, horseradish, salt and pepper in bowl. Fold in mushrooms. Set aside. Cut loaf into halves crosswise. Cut 4 large slices from each half; reserve remaining bread for another purpose. Cut each large bread slice into halves. Spread 1 side of each with mayonnaise. Layer roast beef, sour cream mixture, red pepper rings and watercress over half the bread slices. Top with remaining bread. Cut each into halves. Arrange on serving plate. Yield: 16 sandwiches.

Bobbie D. Smith
Waynoka H.S., Waynoka, OK

Ham Biscuits

2 pkg. dry yeast
2 tbsp. warm water
5 c. self-rising flour
¼ c. sugar
1 c. shortening
2 c. buttermilk
½ c. melted butter
Sliced ham, cut into pieces

Dissolve yeast in water. Mix flour and sugar in bowl. Cut in shortening until crumbly. Add buttermilk and yeast; mix well. Turn onto well-floured surface. Roll to ¼-inch thickness; cut with biscuit cutter. Dip biscuits in butter; place on baking sheet. Bake at 400 degrees for 15 minutes or until golden brown. Place 1 slice ham on each split biscuit. Yield: 3 dozen 2¼-inch or 6 dozen 1¼-inch biscuits.
Note: Dough may be stored in airtight container in refrigerator for up to 1 week. Biscuits may be baked in advance and reheated in microwave at serving time.

Barbara P. Witlen
Richlands Mid. Sch., Richalnds, VA

Traditional Chex Party Mix

½ c. butter
1¼ tsp. seasoned salt
4½ tsp. Worcestershire sauce
2 c. corn Chex
2 c. rice Chex
2 c. bran Chex
2 c. wheat Chex
1 c. salted mixed nuts

Melt butter in large shallow roasting pan in 250-degree oven. Stir in seasoned salt and Worcestershire sauce. Add cereals and nuts; mix gently to coat. Bake for 1 hour, stirring every 15 minutes. Spread on paper towels to cool. Store in airtight container. Yield: 9 cups.
Note: May add pretzel sticks if desired.

Carla Seippel
Fort Osage Jr. H.S., Independence, MO

Trail Mix

2 qt. popped popcorn
1 c. peanuts
1 c. raisins
1 c. coconut
1 c. sunflower seed
1 pkg. M and M's

Combine all ingredients in large bowl; mix well. Pack loosely into clean dry milk cartons, coffee cans with plastic lids, or plastic sandwich bags. Yield: 3 quarts.

Shari Rogers
Lincoln Mid. Sch., Abilene, TX

Glorified Granola

2 c. raisins
2 c. dried banana chips
2 c. chopped dates
2 c. each chopped dried apricots, apples
2 c. carob chips
2 c. chopped cashews
2 c. sunflower seed
2 c. flaked coconut
4 c. granola

Combine all ingredients in large container; mix well. Store in airtight container. Yield: 20 cups.

Judy Wright
Lawton, OK

BEVERAGES

Cider Punch

4 c. orange juice
2 c. lemon juice
8 c. apple cider
2 c. sifted confectioners' sugar

Mix orange juice, lemon juice and cider in pitchers. Stir in confectioners' sugar until dissolved. Pour over ice cubes in glasses. Garnish with mint leaves. Yield: 24 servings.

Yvette Jackson
Nashville, TN

Bodacious Cranberry Punch

1½ c. sugar
4 cinnamon sticks
2 c. water
3 c. cranberry juice
2½ c. orange juice
¾ c. lemon juice
42 oz. lemon-lime soda

Combine sugar, cinnamon sticks and water in saucepan. Simmer for 10 minutes. Let stand for 3 hours to overnight; remove cinnamon. Add fruit juices; mix well. Stir in soda gradually. Pour over ice in punch bowl. Garnish with lime slices. Yield: 35 servings.

William F. Hignett
Baltimore, MD

Cranberry Punch

2 qt. cranberry juice
2   12-oz. cans frozen lemonade
*   concentrate*
6   12-oz. cans water

Combine cranberry juice, lemonade concentrate and water in punch bowl; mix well. Garnish with lemon slices. Ladle into punch cups.
Yield: 1¼ gallons.
Note: May prepare ice ring at least 1 day ahead by freezing additional cranberry juice and lemon slices or mint leaves in ring mold.

Kathy Thomas
Chickasha Mid. Sch., Chickasha, OK

Holiday Cranberry Punch

1 c. sugar
2 c. water
4 c. cranberry juice
4 cinnamon sticks
12 whole cloves
1½ c. lemon juice
2 c. orange juice
2 c. pineapple juice
1 qt. ginger ale, chilled

Boil sugar and water in saucepan until sugar is dissolved. Add cranberry juice, cinnamon and cloves. Simmer for 5 minutes. Strain and cool. Pour into punch bowl. Stir in juices. Chill in refrigerator. Add ginger ale just before serving. Yield: 25 servings.

Rose H. Alexander
Kanawha, WV

Sparkling Cranberry Punch

4 c. cranberry juice   20 cups
2 c. orange juice   10 cups
1 qt. pineapple juice   1¼ gal
¼ c. lemon juice   1¼ c
1 qt. ginger ale   5 qts

Combine chilled juices in punch bowl; mix well. Stir in ginger ale gently just before serving. Ladle into punch cups. Yield: 20 servings.

Betty Barnes
Beulah Sch., Valley, AL

Evergreen Punch

4 pkg. lemon-lime powdered drink mix
16 c. water
2   48-oz. cans pineapple juice
4 c. sugar
2 qt. ginger ale

Blend powdered drink mix, water, pineapple juice and sugar in punch bowl. Chill in refrigerator. Stir in ginger ale and ice just before serving. Yield: 100 servings.

Jessie Lambert
Cairo, IL

Fruity Punch

1 pkg. strawberry powdered drink mix
1 c. sugar
1   6-oz. can each frozen orange juice
*   and lemonade concentrate*
1   18-oz. can pineapple juice
3½ qt. water
1   22-oz. bottle of ginger ale, chilled

Mix first 6 ingredients in punch bowl. Add ginger ale just before serving. Ladle into punch cups. Yield: 36 servings.

Stacy Parker
Grant, WV

Gelatin Punch

2 sm. packages lemon gelatin
4 c. boiling water
4 c. sugar
4 c. water
1 c. lemon juice
2 c. apple juice
1 46-oz. can each unsweetened pineapple
*   juice, orange juice*
1 tbsp. almond extract
1 gal. water

Dissolve gelatin in boiling water in large container. Bring sugar and 4 cups water to a boil in saucepan, stirring until sugar dissolves. Cool. Add to gelatin with remaining ingredients; mix well. Pour into punch bowl. Ladle into punch cups. Yield: 40 servings.

Lotchia Jones
Jasper, TN

Happy Day Punch

1 c. orange juice
3 c. pineapple juice
½ c. lemon juice
1 c. sugar
2 c. club soda
1   32-oz. bottle of lemon-lime soda

Combine juices and sugar in large container, stirring until sugar dissolves. Chill for several hours. Pour over ice in punch bowl. Add sodas carefully. Yield: 24 servings.

Tammy Ferguson
Ramer, TN

Holiday Punch

3 c. sugar
3 c. water
4 c. cranberry juice cocktail
3 c. lemon juice
2 c. orange juice
2 c. unsweetened pineapple juice
2 qt. ginger ale

Bring sugar and water to a boil in saucepan, stirring until sugar is dissolved. Cool. Combine juices in large container. Add sugar syrup to taste. Chill until serving time. Mix gently with ginger ale in punch bowl at serving time. Ladle into punch cups. Yield: 44 servings.

Kathleen Burchett
Area Supr. of H.E., State Dept. of Ed., Abingdon, VA

Lime Fruit Punch

1   3-oz. package lime gelatin
1 c. sugar
1 c. boiling water
1 c. lemon juice
1   46-oz. can pineapple juice

Dissolve gelatin and sugar in boiling water in large container. Add juices and enough water to measure 1 gallon. Chill until serving time, stirring occasionally. Pour into punch bowl. Ladle into punch cups. Yield: 40 servings.

Bessie Fellives
Greeley, CO

Party Punch For Fifty

2   3-oz. packages cherry gelatin
1 c. sugar
3 c. boiling water
1   46-oz. can pineapple juice
12 oz. frozen lemonade concentrate
1 tbsp. almond extract
2 liters (about) ginger ale

Dissolve gelatin and sugar in boiling water in large container. Cool. Add pineapple juice and lemonade. Chill until serving time. Add remaining ingredients just before serving. Ladle into punch cups. Yield: 50 servings.

Carla Seippel
Fort Osage Jr. H.S., Independence, MO

Party Punch

1   46-oz. can orange-grapefruit juice
1   46-oz. can pineapple juice
1   24-oz. bottle of grape juice
1   12-oz. can frozen lemonade
    concentrate
1   28-oz. bottle of ginger ale

Combine fruit juices in large container. Chill until serving time. Combine with ginger ale in punch bowl just before serving. Garnish with lemon slices. Ladle into punch cups.
Yield: 24 servings.

Ruth Mick
Elizabethton, TN

Pastel Sherbet Cream Punch

5 c. canned pineapple juice
1 qt. lime, lemon or raspberry sherbet,
    softened
1 qt. vanilla ice cream, softened
2   12-oz. bottles sparkling water, chilled

Combine pineapple juice, sherbet and half the ice cream in bowl. Beat until smooth. Mix gently with sparkling water in punch bowl. Scoop remaining ice cream into punch. Ladle into punch cups. Yield: 28 servings.

Photograph for this recipe on page 4.

Quantity Punch

1   8-qt. container presweetened
    drink mix powder
1 qt. boiling water
1   46-oz. can pineapple juice
7 qt. cold water

Dissolve drink mix in boiling water in large container. Stir in pineapple juice and 3 quarts cold water. Chill until serving time. Mix with remaining 4 quarts cold water in punch bowl. Ladle into punch cups. Yield: 80 servings.

Deborah C. Carter
Floyd Co. H.S., Floyd, VA

Rosy Punch For-A-Crowd

1 sm. package cherry gelatin
2 c. boiling water
3 c. sugar
1 lg. can pineapple juice
1   16-oz. bottle of lemon juice
16 c. cold water

Dissolve gelatin in boiling water in large container. Stir in sugar and juices until sugar dissolves. Add cold water; mix well. Pour into punch bowl. Ladle into punch cups.
Yield: 36 servings.

Ann Henderson
Dandridge, TN

Sparkle Punch-For-A-Crowd

1   3-oz. package gelatin
3 c. sugar
2 c. boiling water
2 c. frozen lemon juice, thawed
2 qt. cold water
3 qt. pineapple juice
1   28-oz. bottle of ginger ale

Dissolve gelatin and sugar in boiling water in large container. Add lemon juice and cold water; mix well. Stir in pineapple juice and ginger ale. Pour into punch bowl. Ladle into punch cups.
Yield: 50 servings.

Janet Motlow
Marshall, TX

Three-Fruit Punch

12 oz. frozen orange juice concentrate
12 oz. frozen lemonade concentrate
1   46-oz. can pineapple juice
1 c. sugar
6 c. water
2   12-oz. cans ginger ale, chilled

Combine juice concentrates, pineapple juice, sugar and water in freezer container; mix well. Freeze, tightly covered, until firm. Thaw for 5 hours. Place in punch bowl, stirring with fork to break up chunks. Add ginger ale; mix gently. Ladle into punch cups. Yield: 25 servings.

Dortha Smith
Lewis, WV

Hospitality Tea Punch

15 tea bags
2 qt. boiling water
2 c. sugar
1 qt. orange juice
1½ qt. white grape juice
2 c. lemon juice
1 qt. ginger ale

Steep tea bags in water in stockpot for 3 to 5 minutes; remove tea bags. Cool. Stir in sugar and juices. Add ginger ale at serving time. Serve over ice cubes in glasses. Yield: 2 gallons.

Ruth Irwin
Shawnee H.S., Cape Girardeau, MO

Delicious Golden Tea Punch

3 c. sugar
3 qt. water
1 c. strong tea
12 oz. frozen orange juice concentrate
12 oz. frozen lemonade concentrate
1 lg. can pineapple juice
2 qt. ginger ale

Boil sugar and water in saucepan for 8 minutes. Add tea; chill. Stir in juices. Chill for several hours. Pour into punch bowl. Add ginger ale and ice cubes just before serving. Yield: 50 servings.

Lynn Suggs
Birmingham, AL

French Mint Tea

4 lg. tea bags
Juice and rind of 3 lemons
½ c. fresh mint leaves
2 c. boiling water
2 c. sugar
2 46-oz. cans pineapple juice
4 c. cold water
1½ tsp. vanilla extract
½ tsp. almond extract

Steep tea bags, lemon rind and mint leaves in boiling water in saucepan for 15 minutes. Strain into pitcher. Stir in remaining ingredients. Pour over crushed ice in glasses. Garnish with mint sprigs. Yield: 12-16 servings.

Lucille Herron
Cleveland, TN

Fruit and Tea Punch

3 c. sugar
Juice of 10 lemons
Juice of 2 oranges
1½ c. pineapple juice
4 qt. strong hot tea

Dissolve sugar in fruit juices in large container. Add tea. Serve over crushed ice in glasses. Yield: 20 servings.

Winnie Snead Moore
Dresden, TN

Wedding Punch

48 oz. frozen orange juice concentrate
12 oz. frozen lemonade concentrate
2 46-oz. cans pineapple juice
1 46-oz. can grapefruit juice
½ c. sugar
2 to 4 liters ginger ale

Reconstitute orange juice and lemonade using package directions. Combine with remaining juices and sugar in large container. Mix with ginger ale in punch bowl just before serving. Ladle into punch cups. Yield: 100 servings.

Bettie Jo Smotherman
Smithville, TN

Bride's Pink Punch

3 6-oz. packages strawberry gelatin
6 c. boiling water
6 pkg. unsweetened strawberry drink mix
15 c. sugar
3 gal. water
6 46-oz. cans pineapple juice
60 oz. ginger ale
1½ gal. pineapple sherbet

Dissolve gelatin in 6 cups boiling water in saucepan. Combine drink mix, sugar and 3 gallons water in very large container; mix well. Add gelatin mixture and pineapple juice. Chill until serving time. Mix gently with ginger ale in punch bowl. Scoop sherbet into punch. Garnish with fresh strawberries. Ladle into punch cups. Yield: 200 servings.

Nora Sweat
West Hardin H.S., Elizabethtown, KY

Frozen Wedding Punch

1 lg. package cherry gelatin
3 pkg. cherry drink mix
4 to 5 c. sugar
1   12-oz. can each frozen orange juice
*   and lemonade concentrate*
1   48-oz. can pineapple juice
5½ qt. water
1 qt. ginger ale

Mix gelatin, drink mix and sugar in 2-gallon container. Add lemonade concentrate, orange juice concentrate, pineapple juice and water; mix well. Pour into freezer containers. Freeze until firm. Let thaw at room temperature for 2 to 3 hours or until slushy. Mix gently with ginger ale in punch bowl at serving time. Ladle into punch cups. Yield: 2 gallons.

Ruth Irwin
Shawnee H.S., Cape Girardeau, MO

Ice Cream Punch

1 qt. each vanilla, strawberry ice cream
1   46-oz. can Hawaiian punch
1   46-oz. can pineapple-orange juice
1   46-oz. can cranberry juice
Ginger ale

Place scoops of ice cream into punch bowl. Add mixture of punch and juices. Stir in ginger ale gently. Yield: 25 servings.

Harriette Cohn
Bowling Green, KY

Lime Sherbet Froth

5 qt. milk
1 gal. lime sherbet
8 qt. carbonated grapefruit drink
½ gal. pineapple sherbet

Combine milk and lime sherbet in punch bowl; stir until blended. Stir in grapefruit drink gently. Scoop pineapple sherbet into punch. Serve immediately. Yield: 100 servings.

Marilyn Mancewicz
Ottawa Hills H.S., Grand Rapids, MI

Banana Slush Punch

4 c. sugar
6 c. water
1   12-oz. can each frozen orange juice
*   and lemonade concentrate*
1   46-oz. can pineapple juice
3 to 5 ripe bananas, puréed
4 qt. ginger ale

Bring sugar and water to a boil in large saucepan. Boil for 3 minutes, stirring to dissolve sugar. Cool. Add fruit juices and bananas; mix well. Pour into 1-quart freezer containers. Freeze for 2 days or longer. Thaw required amount at room temperature for 1 to 2 hours or until slushy. Combine with equal part ginger ale in punch bowl. Ladle into punch cups. Yield: 50 servings.

Cinda Stocks
Blue Mound H.S., Moweaqua, IL

Slushy Banana-Fruit Punch

4 c. sugar
6 c. water
6 bananas
1   46-oz. can pineapple juice
2   12-oz. cans frozen orange juice
*   concentrate*
1   12-oz. can frozen lemonade
*   concentrate*
7 liters carbonated lemon-lime drink

Bring sugar and water to a boil in saucepan, stirring until sugar is dissolved. Cool. Process bananas in blender container until smooth. Combine sugar syrup, bananas and juices in large container; mix well. Pour into freezer containers. Freeze until firm. Thaw at room temperature for 1 hour or until slushy. Mix gently with lemon-lime drink in punch bowl just before serving. Ladle into punch cups.
Yield: 100 servings.

Barbara J. Bird
Alma H.S., Alma, MI

Pineapple Slush Punch

3 c. sugar
6 c. water
3   3-oz. packages gelatin
1   46-oz. can pineapple juice
1   3-oz. can frozen lemonade
*   concentrate*
1 oz. almond extract
16½ c. water

Bring sugar and 6 cups water to a boil in stockpot. Add gelatin; mix until sugar and gelatin dissolve. Stir in pineapple juice, lemonade concentrate, almond extract and 16½ cups water; mix well. Pour into ½-gallon freezer containers. Freeze until firm. Thaw at room termerature for 4 hours or until slushy. Place in punch bowl. Ladle into punch cups. Yield: 65 servings.

Debra Hart
Emerson Jr. H.S., Enid, OK

Hot Spicy Apple Juice

1 gal. apple juice
1 qt. water
6 each whole cloves, allspice
3 sticks cinnamon

Pour apple juice and water into 30-cup electric percolator. Place spices in basket. Perk until hot and spicy. Yield: 27-30 servings.

Shirley Henkel
Statesville H.S., Statesville, NC

Hot Cranberry Tea

½ c. red cinnamon candies
1 qt. cranberry juice
2 c. sugar
2 c. water
Juice of 2 oranges
Juice of 2 lemons

Dissolve candies in cranberry juice in saucepan over low heat, stirring constantly. Add sugar and water. Cook until sugar dissolves. Stir in orange and lemon juices and additional water to taste. Tint with food coloring if desired. Yield: 15 servings.

Donna Olive
Paris, TN

Microwave Cranberry Punch

1 qt. cranberry juice
1 qt. apple juice
2 tbsp. lemon juice
2 tbsp. sugar
4   2-in. cinnamon sticks
¾ tsp. whole cloves
1 lemon, thinly sliced

Combine juices, sugar and spices in 3-quart microwave container. Microwave, covered, on High for 20 to 25 minutes; stir. Microwave on Medium for 10 minutes longer. Remove spices with slotted spoon. Add lemon slices. Ladle into punch cups. Yield: 14-16 servings.

Sandra Whaley
North Whitfield Mid. Sch., Dalton, GA

Hot Mocha Punch

2 qt. hot coffee
1 qt. chocolate ice cream
Grated nutmeg

Pour coffee over ice cream in bowl. Beat with wire whisk until smooth. Sprinkle with nutmeg. Ladle into mugs. Yield: 16 servings.

Rocio Lerma
Fort Hancock, TX

Wassail Bowl

24 whole cloves
4 cinnamon sticks
1 gal. apple cider
1 qt. orange juice
1 qt. pineapple juice
1 c. lemon juice
1 c. sugar

Tie spices in cheesecloth bag. Combine with remaining ingredients in stockpot; mix well. Simmer for 10 minutes; remove spices. Serve hot in punch cups. Yield: 1½ gallons.

Emily Lewis
Capitol Hill H.S., Oklahoma City, OK

Hot Chocolate Mix

1 25-oz. package nonfat dry milk powder
1 6-oz. jar nondairy creamer
1 16-oz. box chocolate drink mix
1 c. sugar

Combine all ingredients in bowl; mix well. Store in airtight container. Mix 2 tablespoons mix with 1 cup boiling water for each serving.
Yield: 60 servings.

Marcia Ingram
Lexington H.S., Lexington, TX

Instant Cocoa Mix

8 c. nonfat dry milk powder
4 c. instant chocolate drink mix
2 c. nondairy creamer
1½ c. confectioners' sugar
½ c. sugar
½ c. cocoa
½ tsp. salt

Combine all ingredients in airtight container; mix well. Mix ¼ cup mixture with 1 cup boiling water for each serving. Yield: 64 servings.

Cynthia Kolberg
Fairfield Jr.-Sr. H.S., Goshen, IN

Friendship Tea Mix

1 18-oz. jar orange breakfast drink mix
1 c. sugar
½ c. lemonade mix
½ c. instant tea mix
1 3-oz. package apricot-flavored gelatin
2½ tsp. cinnamon
1 tsp. cloves

Combine all ingredients; mix well. Store in airtight container. Combine 1½ tablespoons tea mixture with 1 cup hot water for each serving. Yield: 75 servings.

Norma Shaffer
Isanti, MN

Spiced Tea Mix

1 4-oz. jar low-calorie lemon tea mix
2 c. orange breakfast drink mix
1½ tsp. ground cloves
3 tsp. cinnamon
1 tsp. allspice
3 to 5 cinnamon sticks

Combine all ingredients except cinnamon sticks in large bowl; mix well. Store, tightly covered, in jar with cinnamon sticks in center. Mix 2 teaspoons mixture with 1 cup hot water for each serving. Yield: 75 servings.

Karen Jones
Pawnee, TX

Lemonade Mix

4 lemons
2 c. sugar
½ c. water

Cut lemons in half. Squeeze lemons and mash pulp into sugar in bowl. Stir in water. Let stand for 1 hour; strain. Place 1 or 2 tablespoons mixture in each glass. Fill glasses with ice and water. Yield: 12 servings.

Louise Lile
Nashville, TN

Easy Golden Punch

12 oz. frozen orange juice concentrate
12 oz. frozen lemonade concentrate
1 12-oz. can apricot nectar
1 46-oz. can pineapple juice
2½ qt. cold water
2 qt. orange sherbet, softened
1 qt. ginger ale, chilled

Mix orange juice and lemonade concentrates with apricot nectar and pineapple juice in large container. Chill in refrigerator. Pour over ice in punch bowl. Add water, sherbet and ginger ale just before serving. Yield: 40 servings.

Elsie Latham
Shreveport, LA

SOUPS
AND
STEWS

Bean Soup

3 c. dried mixed beans, washed
5 qt. water
2 lb. ham, chopped
2 lg. onions
6 cloves of garlic
2 cans Ro-Tel tomatoes
Juice of 2 lemons
Salt and pepper to taste

Soak beans in water to cover for 3 hours to overnight; drain. Combine beans with 5 quarts water in stockpot. Simmer, covered, for 1½ hours. Add ham, onions and garlic. Simmer, covered, for 2 hours. Stir in remaining ingredients. Simmer for 30 minutes longer.
Yield: 15-20 servings.

Kevin Chadwick
Amarillo, TX

Cheese-Broccoli Soup

25 lb. potatoes, peeled, chopped
5 lg. onions, chopped
5 lb. carrots, shredded
6 lb. broccoli, chopped
6 c. cooked corn
Milk
6 lb. American cheese, cubed

Combine potatoes, onions, carrots, broccoli and water to cover in large stockpot. Simmer until tender; drain. Add corn, enough milk to cover vegetables and cheese. Cook until cheese melts, stirring frequently. Thicken with flour and water paste if desired. Yield: 50 servings.

Ginny Stutler
Jefferson, VA

Cheddar Cheese Soup

½ c. each chopped celery, green pepper,
* onion, carrot and cauliflower*
½ c. margarine
2 c. water
2 chicken bouillon cubes
½ c. melted margarine
⅔ c. flour
4 c. milk
8 oz. Cheddar cheese, grated

Sauté vegetables in ½ cup margarine in large saucepan. Add water and bouillon cubes. Bring to a boil; reduce heat. Simmer, covered, for 10 minutes. Blend melted margarine and flour in saucepan. Cook until bubbly. Stir in milk gradually. Cook over medium heat until thickened, stirring constantly. Stir in cheese until melted. Pour into vegetable mixture; mix well. Yield: 14 servings.

Deon LaBathe
Hudsonville H.S., Hudsonville, MI

Cheddar Cheese and Ham Soup

1 c. each finely chopped onion,
* carrot and celery*
½ c. margarine
1 c. flour
4 c. chicken stock
3 c. grated Cheddar cheese
1 c. chopped cooked ham
¾ c. chopped cooked potato
1½ qt. milk
1 tsp. salt
½ tsp. white pepper

Sauté onion, carrot and celery in margarine in large saucepan. Sprinkle with flour. Add chicken stock. Cook until smooth, stirring constantly. Simmer for 15 minutes. Stir in cheese. Cook for 10 minutes longer. Add remaining ingredients. Heat to serving temperature. Yield: 12 servings.

Judy Stephan
Dover, TN

Cream of Chicken Soup

¾ c. melted margarine
¾ c. flour
1½ c. each milk, light cream
6 c. chicken broth
6 c. finely chopped cooked chicken
1 tsp. salt
¼ tsp. pepper

Blend margarine and flour in large saucepan. Stir in milk, cream and broth gradually. Cook until thickened and bubbly, stirring constantly. Add chicken and seasonings. Heat to serving temperature. Ladle into soup bowls. Garnish with minced chives or parsley. Yield: 12-15 servings.

Nancy B. Womack
Botetourt Vo. Sch., Fincastle, VA

Clam Chowder

2 c. minced clams
2 bottles of clam juice
1   13-oz. can chicken broth
½ lb. salt pork, chopped
1 c. chopped onion
3 c. chopped peeled potatoes
1 tsp. salt
¼ tsp. white pepper
2 c. light cream
2 c. milk
2 tbsp. butter
¼ tsp. paprika

Drain clams, reserving liquid. Combine clam juice, reserved clam liquid, broth and enough water to measure 4 cups; set aside. Fry salt pork in skillet until golden. Remove pork and drain, reserving ¼ cup drippings. Sauté onion in reserved drippings for 5 minutes. Combine onion, clam juice mixture, potatoes, salt and pepper in large saucepan. Cook over low heat until potatoes are tender. Add cream, milk, butter and clams. Cook for 3 minutes or until heated through. Do not boil. Sprinkle with paprika. Ladle into soup bowls. Yield: 12-15 servings.
Note: Flavor imporves if made 1 day ahead.

Trudy Noble
Rusk, TX

Gulf Shores Clam Chowder

⅓ c. diced salt pork
½ c. finely chopped onion
3 c. sliced potatoes
2 c. hot water
1 tsp. salt
⅛ tsp. pepper
2   10-oz. cans minced clams
3 c. milk

Fry salt pork in 4-quart saucepan until golden brown; remove and reserve crisp bits. Sauté onion in drippings. Add potatoes, water and seasonings. Simmer, covered, for 15 minutes. Add clams with clam liquid and milk. Bring just to the boiling point. Do not boil. Ladle into soup bowls. Sprinkle with reserved bits.
Yield: 10-15 servings.

Hassie Hunter Green
Goshen H.S., Goshen, AL

Gazpacho

4 med. cucumbers, peeled
7 stalks celery
2 med. green peppers
2 med. yellow onions
8 lg. cloves of garlic
6 lg. tomatoes, peeled
1 bunch green onions
1¼ c. olive oil
¼ c. vinegar
Juice of 6 lemons
½ tsp. garlic salt
2 tbsp. salt
4½ tsp. pepper
3   12-oz. cans (or more) V-8 juice
3   12-oz. cans spicy hot V-8 juice
1   12-oz. can tomato juice
1   12-oz. bottle of clamato juice
2 tbsp. Worcestershire sauce
½ tsp. Tabasco sauce

Chop cucumbers, celery, green peppers, yellow onions, garlic, tomatoes and green onions coarsely in food processor. Place in 12-quart dish. Add olive oil, vinegar, lemon juice, garlic salt, salt and pepper; mix well. Let stand for 15 minutes. Stir in juices, Worcestershire and Tabasco sauces and enough additional V-8 juice to make of desired consistency. Chill for 24 hours or longer to improve flavor. Garnish with parsley sprigs and lemon slices.
Yield: 30-50 servings.
To make aspic: Combine 2 cups Gazpacho to 1 envelope unflavored gelatin dissolved according to package directions. Pour into mold. Chill in refrigerator until firm. Unmold on lettuce-lined serving plate.

Martha Goucher
Denver, CO

Microwave Gazpacho

1 cucumber, peeled, chopped
4 tomatoes, peeled, finely chopped
⅓ c. chopped onion
1 clove of garlic, minced
½ c. each finely chopped green pepper,
*   celery, zucchini, yellow squash*
½ c. finely shredded carrot
2 cans cream of celery soup
2 soup cans water

Combine vegetables in glass bowl. Blend soup and water in small bowl. Stir into vegetable mixture. Microwave until heated through. Cool. Chill for 4 hours to overnight. Serve in chilled bowls. Garnish with freshly ground pepper and chopped parsley. Yield: 12 servings.

Jean Turk
Wheaton North H.S., Wheaton, IL

Marvelous Minestrone Soup

3 qt. beef broth
1 c. tomato sauce
1 tbsp. salt
3 potatoes, chopped
3 onions, chopped
¼ head cabbage, chopped
1   10-oz. package frozen green beans
1   10-oz. package frozen chopped
*   spinach*
1 c. chopped celery
4 oz. shell macaroni, cooked
1   16-oz. can kidney beans
2 tbsp. brown sugar
3 tbsp. butter
3 tbsp. Parmesan cheese
¼ c. Burgundy
1 clove of garlic, finely chopped

Combine broth, tomato sauce, salt, potatoes and next 5 ingredients in stockpot. Cook over low heat until vegetables are tender. Add remaining ingredients. Cook for 10 minutes longer. Yield: 20 servings.

Clarisse Boomer
St. Louis, MO

Mulligatawny Soup

1 sm. eggplant, chopped
2 green peppers, chopped
3 apples, peeled, chopped
2 lg. onions, chopped
1 bunch celery, chopped
¾ c. margarine
1 c. flour
3 tbsp. curry powder
Salt to taste
1 tsp. white pepper
2 c. hot chicken stock
2 gal. hot milk
1½ qt. light cream
1½ c. cooked rice
2 c. chopped cooked chicken

Blanch eggplant in boiling salted water for 5 minutes; drain. Blanch green peppers and apples together in boiling salted water for 5 minutes; drain. Sauté onions and celery in margarine in 4-gallon stockpot. Add flour and seasonings. Cook over low heat for 5 to 6 minutes, stirring frequently; do not brown. Stir in stock gradually. Cook until thickened, stirring constantly. Bring to a boil. Add eggplant, green peppers and apples. Simmer until vegetables are tender. Stir in remaining ingredients. Heat to serving temperature. Adjust seasonings.

Kathy Thomas
Chickasha Mid. Sch., Chickasha, OK

Creamed Spinach Soup

1 chopped onion
¼ c. margarine
⅔ c. flour
¼ tsp. nutmeg
5 c. milk
1½ c. cubed Velveeta cheese
2   10-oz. packages frozen spinach,
*   thawed*

Sauté onion in margarine in skillet until tender. Stir in flour and nutmeg. Stir in milk and 1 cup water gradually. Simmer until thickened, stirring constantly. Add cheese and spinach. Cook until cheese is melted, stirring frequently. Yield: 20 servings.

Dorothy Hunt
Crawfordsville, GA

Gourmet Prairie Pasta Soup

4 oz. each spinach noodles,
  rotini, shell macaroni
½ c. sliced green onions
1 c. shredded carrots,
1 c. sliced mushrooms
1 c. chopped broccoli
3 tbsp. butter
2½ c. milk
3 tbsp. flour
3 tbsp. melted butter
¾ tsp. seasoned salt
½ tsp. lemon pepper
½ c. milk
3 tbsp. instant chicken bouillon
1 c. boiling water
1 c. shredded Cheddar cheese
1 c. Parmesan cheese

Cook each pasta just until tender, according to package directions; drain and set aside. Sauté vegetables in 3 tablespoons butter in heavy 2-quart saucepan until tender. Stir in 2½ cups milk. Blend flour, 3 tablespoons butter, seasonings and ½ cup milk in small bowl. Stir into vegetable mixture. Add bouillon dissolved in boiling water. Cook until bubbly, stirring constantly. Add pasta and cheeses. Cook until cheese melts, stirring gently. Serve immediately. Yield: 12 servings.

Cathy Mitchell
Clinton H.S., Clinton, MO

Cabbage-Potato Soup

3 qt. water
3 tbsp. salt
3 med. onions, chopped
8 med. potatoes, peeled, quartered
1½ lb. cabbage, shredded
3 tbsp. butter

Combine water, salt and onions in large saucepan. Bring to a boil. Add potatoes. Cook until tender. Remove and mash potatoes; return to saucepan. Add cabbage and butter. Simmer for 20 to 30 minutes. Yield: 12 servings.

Gail Dixon
Lyons Jr HS, Vidalia, GA

Homemade Vegetable-Beef Soup

1 lb. chuck roast, cubed
2 tbsp. oil
1 lg. can tomatoes
2 tsp. salt
Pepper to taste
Dash each of basil, red pepper
3 c. water
3 med. potatoes, peeled, diced
4 lg. carrots, peeled, diced
1 lg. onion, chopped
1 16-oz. can whole kernel corn
2 c. mixed vegetables

Brown beef in oil in 5-quart saucepan. Add tomatoes, seasonings and water. Simmer until beef is nearly tender. Stir in potatoes, carrots and onion. Cook until beef and vegetables are tender. Add remaining ingredients. Simmer for 30 to 45 minutes longer, adding 1 cup additional water if necessary. Yield: 12 servings.

Bonnie Vickers
Bolivar, PA

French Onion Soup

10 yellow onions, thinly sliced
1 stick butter
1 qt. water
2 tbsp. instant beef bouillon
2 tbsp. Sherry
Salt to taste
Freshly ground pepper to taste
French bread, sliced, toasted
Mozzarella cheese, shredded

Sauté onions in butter in stockpot until tender. Add water and bouillon. Simmer for 45 minutes. Stir in Sherry, salt and pepper. Ladle into serving bowls. Top with bread and cheese. Broil until cheese melts. Yield: 12 servings.

Giselle Kraft
Austin, TX

Texas Red Chili

6 tbsp. chili powder
1 tbsp. each oregano, cumin and salt
1 tsp. cayenne pepper (opt.)
1 29-oz. can tomato juice
3 29-oz. cans hot chili beans
4 c. water
3 lb. ground beef

Combine seasonings, juice, beans and water in large saucepan. Simmer for several minutes. Brown ground beef in skillet, stirring frequently. Add to bean mixture. Cook over low heat for 1 hour. Thin with additional tomato juice or thicken with flour or cornstarch to make of desired consistency. Yield: 15 servings.

Tammy Walls
Decherd, TX

Brick Chili

10 lb. ground beef
4 to 5 cloves of garlic, minced
2 tbsp. salt
2 tsp. oregano
2 tsp. cumin
2 tsp. coriander
1 tsp. anise
2 6-oz. cans tomato paste
2 to 3 tbsp. chili powder
1½ c. flour

Brown ground beef in stockpot, stirring until crumbly. Add garlic and next 4 seasonings; mix well. Cook for 45 to 60 minutes. Drain, reserving drippings. Add tomato paste and chili powder; mix well. Blend flour with reserved drippings; stir into ground beef mixture. Cook for 10 to 15 minutes, stirring constantly. Pour into large pan. Chill overnight. Cut into desired size bricks. Store, tightly covered, in freezer. Place chili brick in saucepan. Add enough water to make of desired consistency. Simmer for 20 to 30 minutes, adding beans if desired.
Yield: 20-40 servings.

Cheryl Zimmerman
Pittsfield H.S., Griggsville, IL

Chili

6 lb. coarsely ground beef
1 c. chili powder

2 tbsp. oregano
2 tbsp. cumin
2 tbsp. salt
2 tbsp. garlic powder
2 qt. water
½ c. yellow cornmeal
1 lb. smoked sausage, cubed

Brown ground beef in large saucepan, stirring until crumbly; drain. Add spices; mix well. Stir in water. Bring to a boil; reduce heat. Simmer for 2 hours. Stir in cornmeal. Add a small amount of additional water if necessary to make of desired consistency. Add sausage. Simmer for 30 minutes. Yield: 24 servings.
Note: May be halved.

Sharon Ledgerwood
Moore H.S., Moore, OK

Chili For One Hundred

30 lb. ground beef
12 No. 10 cans tomato juice
12 No. 10 cans beans
20 c. elbow macaroni, cooked
¾ c. dried onions
2½ c. chili powder
Salt and pepper to taste

Brown ground beef in large skillets, stirring until crumbly; drain. Add remaining ingredients; mix well. Simmer until flavors are blended.
Yield: 100 servings.

Mary Jane Smith
Pleasant View Jr. H.S., Richmond, IN

Quick Ground Beef Stew

4 lb. ground beef
2 c. chopped onions
2 green peppers, chopped
8 cans vegetable soup
Salt and pepper to taste

Brown ground beef with onion and green pepper in stockpot, stirring until crumbly. Stir in soup and salt and pepper. Heat to serving temperature, stirring frequently. Yield: 12 servings.

Dorothy Kunkle
Friendswood, TX

Beef Stew

5 lb. beef stew meat
5 lb. potatoes, peeled, cubed
1 lb. carrot chunks
3 onions, quartered
5 stalks celery, sliced
½ tsp. Worcestershire sauce
1 tbsp. salt
½ tsp. pepper
½ c. minute tapioca
2 cans tomato soup
2 soup cans water

Layer stew meat, vegetables, seasonings, tapioca, soup and water in 12x24-inch oval roaster. Bake, covered, at 275 degrees for 5 hours. Stir gently before serving. Yield: 18-20 servings.

Jayne Garber
East Clinton H.S., Sabina, OH

Old-Fashioned Stew

2 lb. stew beef
6 c. water
4 c. chopped carrots
4 c. chopped potaotes
1 c. chopped onion
2 bay leaves
Salt and pepper to taste

Brown stew beef in a small amount of shortening in skillet. Add water. Simmer, covered, for 2 hours. Add remaining ingredients. Simmer for 1 hour longer. Remove bay leaves. May thicken if desired. Yield: 12 servings.

Hazel Johnson
Pavillion, WY

Brunswick Stew

1 5 to 6-lb. chicken
2 lb. lean pork, cubed
6 med. onions
6 med. potatoes
3 28-oz. cans tomatoes
2 16-oz. cans lima beans
2 16-oz. cans corn
3 tbsp. Worcestershire sauce
Salt and pepper to taste

Cook chicken in water to cover in 10-quart stockpot until tender. Remove and bone chicken. Skim broth. Add pork and onions to broth. Cook until tender. Cook potatoes and tomatoes in saucepan until potatoes are tender, stirring frequently to prevent scorching. Add tomato mixture to broth mixture. Add lima beans, corn and seasonings. Simmer for several hours, stirring occasionally to prevent scorching. Yield: 20 servings.
Note: This stew freezes well.

Lois H. Webber
East Forsyth H.S., Kernersville, NC

Easy Brunswick Stew

2 14-oz. cans chicken broth
3 16-oz. cans cream-style corn
3 16-oz. cans tomatoes
3 17-oz. cans early English peas
Salt and pepper to taste
2 c. chopped cooked chicken or pork
8 to 12 oz. saltine crackers, crumbled

Combine broth and vegetables in large saucepan. Add salt and pepper. Simmer for 3 to 4 hours. Stir in chicken. Add enough cracker crumbs to make of desired consistency. Yield: 20 servings.

Gail Helms
Enterprise H.S., Enterprise, AL

Quick Brunswick Stew

1 28-oz. can tomatoes
½ c. chopped onion
2 10-oz. cans barbecued chicken
1 16-oz. can barbecued pork
1 10-oz. can barbecued beef
1 10-oz. can whole kernel corn
1 10-oz. can cream-style corn
2 tbsp. Worcestershire sauce
Soy sauce and Tabasco sauce to taste
1 tbsp. lemon juice
Salt and pepper to taste

Purée tomatoes in blender. Combine all ingredients in large saucepan. Simmer for 15 minutes or until onion is tender, stirring frequently. Yield: 12 servings.

Anne Meeks
Beauregard H.S., Opelika, AL

Camp Stew for Two Hundred

10 lg. chickens
15 lb. ground beef
20 lb. ground pork
6 gal. chopped peeled potatoes
2 gal. chopped onions
10 qt. peas
12 qt. lima beans
10 qt. corn
10 gal. tomatoes
2½ lb. butter
Hot sauce to taste
Salt and pepper to taste

Cook chickens in water to cover in large stockpot. Remove chickens; reserve broth. Bone and chop chickens. Cook ground beef and pork in large stockpot until brown and crumbly. Add chicken, broth and remaining ingredients. Simmer for 4 hours, stirring very frequently. Yield: 200 servings.

Mrs. Clarence M. Williams
Liberty, NC

Crazy Stew

1 lb. ground beef
1 c. chopped onion
1   10-oz. can corn
1 c. cooked brown beans
1   10-oz. can pork and beans
¼ c. packed brown sugar
1 c. chopped potatoes
⅛ tsp. each salt, pepper
½ tsp. garlic salt
1 c. each catsup, tomato juice
1 tbsp. liquid smoke
3 tbsp. white vinegar

Brown ground beef and onion in skillet; drain. Place in 6-quart Crock•Pot. Add remaining ingredients 1 at a time, mixing well after each addition. Cook on Low for 2 hours or to desired consistency. Yield: 12 servings.

Mary Connors
West Memphis, AR

Pot Luck Stew

2 lb. ground beef
1 onion, chopped
2   8-oz. cans tomato sauce
2 lg. potatoes, cubed
2 beef bouillon cubes
2 bay leaves
Pepper and finely chopped parsley
*   to taste*
8   8-oz. cans vegetables

Brown ground beef and onion in skillet, stirring until crumbly; drain. Stir in remaining ingredients. Simmer, covered, for 1 hour or longer. Serve with French bread or corn bread. This is a good group-cooking meal. Allow ¼ pound ground beef per person. Ask each person to furnish 1 can of vegetables of any kind suitable for stew and a favorite fresh fruit for fruit bowl. The stew will never be the same twice.

Jennifer Scott
Canadian, OK

Veal Ragoût

4 slices bacon
2 lg. onions, sliced
6 green onions, chopped
6 tbsp. butter
4 lb. veal, cut into 1½-inch cubes
¼ c. flour
1 tbsp. salt
½ tsp. pepper
¼ tsp. oregano
1 c. water
2 c. sour cream

Cut bacon into 1-inch pieces. Sauté in heavy skillet until cooked but not brown. Add onions and butter. Sauté until onions are partially cooked. Coat veal with mixture of flour and seasonings. Add to skillet. Sauté until brown. Add water. Simmer, covered, for 1 hour or until veal is tender. Do not allow to scorch. Push veal to side. Blend sour cream into drippings. Mix in veal. Simmer, covered, for 15 minutes. Garnish with chopped parsley or chives. Yield: 12 servings.

Emma Ellen Bunyard
Jenks H.S., Jenks, OK

Lobster Stew

1 c. each chopped onion, green pepper
  and celery
3 tbsp. butter
6 c. chicken broth
1 28-oz. can tomatoes
Salt and pepper to taste
2 c. small pasta shells
8 c. chopped cooked lobster
12 c. torn fresh spinach leaves

Sauté onion, green pepper and celery in butter in saucepan until tender; do not brown. Add chicken broth, tomatoes, salt and pepper. Bring to a boil. Add pasta. Simmer until pasta is tender. Add lobster and spinach. Heat to serving temperature. Serve over rice. Yield: 12 servings.

Luella Clark
Solway, NY

Microwave Gumbo

½ c. flour
½ c. oil
¼ c. chopped green pepper
1 onion, chopped
2 stalks celery, chopped
1 10-oz. package frozen okra
2 cloves of garlic, minced
¼ c. oil
2 c. chicken broth
1 12-oz. can tomato juice
4 c. water
1 c. each chopped cooked chicken, ham
1 tbsp. Worcestershire sauce
½ tsp. liquid crab boil
1 tsp. pepper
¼ tsp. cayenne pepper
1 tbsp. salt
2 bay leaves
¼ tsp. each rosemary, thyme
1 tbsp. parsley flakes
1½ lb. shrimp, peeled
½ to 1 lb. crab meat

Blend flour and ½ cup oil in 2-cup glass measure. Microwave on High for 4 to 6 minutes or to desired browness for roux, stirring every 2 minutes. Combine vegetables, garlic and ¼ cup oil in 4-quart glass casserole. Microwave on Medium for 7 to 8 minutes or until vegetables are tender, stirring occasionally. Stir in roux, broth, tomato juice, water, chicken, ham and seasonings. Microwave on High for 10 to 12 minutes. Stir in shrimp and crab meat. Microwave on High for 5 to 6 minutes. Remove bay leaves. Serve over rice. Yield: 14 servings.

Linda Finley
Harrison Central Ninth Gr. Sch., Gulfport, MS

Mississippi Seafood Gumbo

¼ c. oil
¼ c. margarine
1¼ c. flour
1 lb. okra, sliced ¼ inch thick
1 lg. onion, finely chopped
2 cloves of garlic, minced
3 stalks celery, finely chopped
1 med. green pepper, finely chopped
1 16-oz. can tomato sauce
1 16-oz. can peeled tomatoes
1 tbsp. Worcestershire sauce
Tabasco sauce to taste
Salt and pepper to taste
1 lb. crab meat
2 lb. peeled shrimp

Heat oil and margarine in large heavy saucepan. Add flour gradually. Cook over medium heat until dark brown, stirring constantly. Add okra. Cook until coated, stirring constantly. Add onion, garlic, celery and green pepper. Cook until coated, stirring constantly. Add tomato sauce, tomatoes and seasonings. Simmer for 1 hour or longer, stirring occasionally. Add seafood. Cook for 10 minutes or just until shrimp turn pink. Let stand for several minutes to blend flavors. Reheat and serve over rice. Yield: 12 servings. Note: This freezes well and can be doubled.

Kirby McHenry
Pascagoula H.S., Gautier, MS

Seafood Gumbo

1 c. bacon drippings
1 c. flour
1 stalk celery, chopped
1 white onion, chopped
2 bunches green onions, chopped
1 green pepper, chopped
8 oz. okra, chopped
3 cloves of garlic, chopped
2   15-oz. cans tomato sauce
4 tomato sauce cans water
1 tbsp. sugar
1 tbsp. parsley
1 tbsp. red pepper
1 tsp. salt
4 bay leaves
2 qt. boiling water
2 lb. cleaned shrimp
1 lb. lump crab meat
1 lb. crab claws
Hot sauce to taste

Blend bacon drippings and flour in enamel stockpot. Sauté over very low heat for 1 hour or until brown. Add celery, onion, green onions, green pepper, okra and garlic. Sauté for 10 minutes. Stir in tomato sauce, 4 sauce cans water and seasonings. Simmer for 10 minutes. Add boiling water, shrimp, crab meat and crab claws. Simmer for 1 hour or longer. Season with hot sauce. Serve over rice in soup bowls. Yield: 12 servings.
Note: Flavor improves if prepared 1 day before. May be stored in freezer for 1 to 2 months.

Elaine Graff
Sun City, FL

Seafood-Sausage Gumbo

1½ c. oil
1½ c. flour
2 c. chopped celery
2 green peppers, chopped
2 onions, minced
3 cloves of garlic, minced
1 lb. smoked sausage, sliced
1 No. 10 can tomatoes, chopped
2 to 3 qt. water
2 bay leaves
¼ c. chopped parsley
1 lb. okra, sliced

½ c. oil
5 lb. peeled shrimp
2 lb. crab meat
¼ c. filé gumbo

Brown flour in 1½ cups oil in skillet until cinnamon-colored, stirring constantly. Add celery, green peppers, onions, garlic and sausage. Cook until tender, stirring constantly. Place in 9-quart stockpot. Stir in tomatoes and water gradually. Add bay leaves and parsley. Sauté okra in ½ cup oil in skillet until tender. Add to stockpot. Simmer for 2 hours. Add shrimp, crab meat and filé. Cook for 30 minutes longer. Serve over rice. Yield: 25 servings.
Note: Be cautious; the roux burns easily.

Sharon Coward
Ocean Springs, H.S., Ocean Springs, MS

Jambalaya

1½ c. chopped pork
1 c. chopped green onions
1 c. chopped onion
1 c. chopped celery
1 c. chopped green pepper
3 tbsp. butter
9 lg. tomatoes, chopped
2   6-oz. cans tomato paste
2 cloves of garlic, minced
½ tsp. thyme
Tabasco sauce to taste
3 bay leaves
¼ tsp. red pepper
1 tsp. salt
Pepper to taste
2 c. chicken broth
1½ lb. shrimp, chopped

Sauté pork, onions, celery and green pepper in butter in large saucepan. Stir in tomatoes, tomato paste, garlic, seasonings and broth. Simmer for 30 minutes. Add shrimp and additional green pepper and celery if desired. Simmer for 30 minutes longer, adding water as necessary to make of desired consistency. Serve over generous servings of hot fluffy rice in soup bowls. Yield: 12 servings.

Shirley Terry
Nashville, TN

SALADS

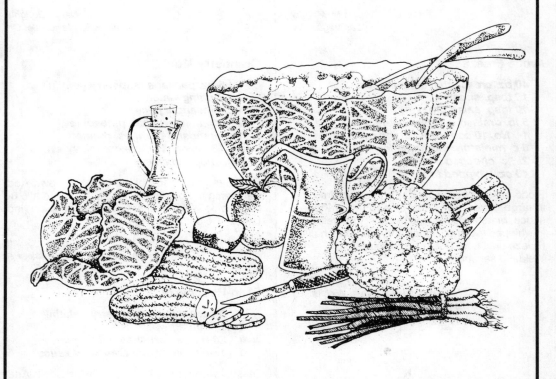

Ambrosia Salad

1 pt. strawberries, sliced
2 bananas, sliced
2 apples, sliced
1 8-oz. can pineapple chunks, drained
1 12-oz. can mandarin oranges, drained
1 16-oz. can fruit cocktail, drained
1 8-oz. package walnuts
1 8-oz. package almonds
2 pkg. whipped topping mix, prepared

Combine fruits and half the nuts in large bowl; mix well. Mix in half the whipped topping. Spread remaining whipped topping over top. Sprinkle with remaining nuts. Yield: 15-20 servings.

Joann M. Murphy
Las Vegas, NV

Arctic Freeze

40 oz. cream cheese, softened
10 tbsp. sugar
10 tbsp. salad dressing
5 lb. drained crushed pineapple
1 No. 10 can whole cranberry sauce
5 c. miniature marshmallows
2½ c. chopped pecans
40 oz. whipped topping

Blend cream cheese, sugar and salad dressing in large mixer bowl. Add pineapple, cranberry sauce, marshmallows and pecans; mix well. Fold in whipped topping. Spoon into 12x20-inch dish. Freeze until firm. Cut into squares. Yield: 50 servings.

Fonda Wren
Wichita H.S. West, Wichita, KS

Thanksgiving Tart Cherry Jell-O

1 16-oz. can tart cherries
1 16-oz. can crushed pineapple
1 lg. package cherry gelatin
¼ c. orange juice
2 tbsp. lemon juice
¼ c. chopped celery
¼ c. chopped nuts

Drain cherries and pineapple, reserving 1½ cups liquid. Bring reserved liquid to a boil in saucepan. Add gelatin; stir until dissolved. Stir in orange juice and lemon juice. Chill until partially set. Add fruit, celery and nuts; mix well. Pour into 2-quart bowl. Chill until set. Yield: 12 servings.

Nancy Doughty
Newcastle H.S., Newcastle, OK

Cranberry Mold

1 6-oz. package raspberry gelatin
2 c. boiling water
1 c. pineapple juice
2 c. drained crushed pineapple
1 c. mandarin oranges, drained
2 16-oz. cans whole cranberry sauce
1 c. chopped celery

Dissolve gelatin in boiling water in bowl. Add remaining ingredients; mix well. Pour into two 6-cup molds. Chill until set. Unmold onto serving plates. Yield: 20 servings.

Esther Gelatt
Honesdale H.S., Honesdale, PA

Cran-Raspberry Mold

1 6-oz. package raspberry gelatin
1¾ c. boiling water
1 20-oz. can crushed pineapple
1 16-oz. can whole cranberry sauce

Dissolve gelatin in boiling water in bowl. Add undrained pineapple and cranberry sauce; mix until cranberry sauce melts. Chill until partially set; mix well. Spoon into 6½-cup ring mold. Chill until set. Unmold onto serving plate. Yield: 12 servings.

Sybil B. Murphy
Northwood H.S., Pittsboro, NC

Glazed Fruit Salad

1   20-oz. can pineapple chunks
1   30-oz. can fruit cocktail
2   11-oz. cans mandarin oranges
7 or 8 bananas, sliced
2 tbsp. lemon juice
1   22-oz. can apricot or peach pie filling

Drain canned fruits. Combine canned fruits, bananas and lemon juice in bowl. Fold in pie filling. Chill overnight. Yield: 12 servings.

Betty K. Munsey
Bland H.S., Bland, VA

Orange Jell-O Salad

1   15-oz. can fruit cocktail,
    partially drained
1   15-oz. can crushed pineapple, drained
½ pkg. miniature marshmallows
Chopped nuts
Coconut
1   3-oz. package orange gelatin
1   8-oz. carton whipped topping

Combine fruit cocktail, pineapple, marshmallows, nuts and coconut in bowl; mix well. Sprinkle with gelatin. Fold in whipped topping. Chill in refrigerator. Yield: 15 servings.

Lavern Frentzel
Perry Co. Dist. 32 Sch., Uniontown, MO

Frosted Orange Salad

1   6-oz. package orange gelatin
2 c. boiling water
1 c. orange juice
1 c. cold water
1 c. drained mandarin oranges
1 c. drained crushed pineapple
1   3-oz. package lemon instant
    pudding mix
1 c. cold water
1 pkg. whipped topping mix

Dissolve gelatin in boiling water in bowl. Stir in orange juice and 1 cup cold water. Chill until partially set. Stir in oranges and pineapple. Pour into 9x13-inch dish. Chill until firm. Combine pudding mix and 1 cup cold water in bowl. Beat

for 1 minute. Prepare topping mix according to package directions. Fold into pudding. Spread on congealed layer. Chill for 1 hour or longer. Cut into squares. Yield: 24 servings.

Carolyn Bailey
Shepherd Pub. Sch., Shepherd, MI

Frozen Butter Mint Salad

1   3-oz. package lime gelatin
1   10-oz. package miniature
    marshmallows
1   20-oz. can crushed pineapple
1 lg. carton whipped topping
1   8-oz. package butter mints, chopped
1 tbsp. lemon juice

Mix dry gelatin, marshmallows and pineapple in bowl. Chill, covered, for 6 hours to overnight. Add whipped topping, butter mints and lemon juice; mix well. Spread evenly in 9x13-inch dish. Freeze until firm. Cut into squares.
Yield: 20 servings.
Note: May spoon into paper-lined muffin cups, freeze and store in plastic bag in freezer.

Jean Holbrook
Supervisor of H.E., Roanoke Co. Sch., Salem, VA

Strawberry Salad Deluxe

1 lg. package strawberry gelatin
1 c. boiling water
2   10-oz. packages frozen strawberries,
    thawed
1   20-oz. can crushed pineapple, drained
1 c. walnuts
3 lg. bananas, mashed
1 pt. sour cream

Dissolve gelatin in boiling water. Fold in strawberries with juice, drained pineapple, walnuts and mashed bananas. Chill until partially set. Pour ⅓ of the mixture into 8x12-inch dish. Layer sour cream and remaining strawberry mixture ½ at a time in prepared dish. Chill until firm. May be served in large crystal bowl.
Yield: 18 servings.

Paula Wingo
Old Greenwich, CT

Bunny Bowl

4 lb. carrots, cut into strips
1 bunch celery, cut into strips
2 pt. cherry tomatoes
1 lg. cucumber, cut into ¼-in. slices
1 lg. green pepper, cut into strips

Combine all ingredients in large bowl; mix well. Yield: 10-20 servings.

Carla Townsend
Philadelphia, PA

Marinated Broccoli

1 c. cider vinegar
1½ c. oil
1 tbsp. sugar
1 tbsp. dillweed
1 tbsp. MSG
1 tsp. each salt, garlic salt
1 tsp. coarsely ground pepper (opt.)
Flowerets of 3 bunches broccoli

Combine first 8 ingredients in large bowl; mix well. Add broccoli. Chill, covered, for 24 hours, stirring occasionally. Drain; place in serving bowl. Garnish with thin slices of fresh orange. Yield: 15-20 servings.

Jean Holbrook
Supervisor of H.E., Roanoke Co. Sch., Salem, VA

Reunion Coleslaw

10 heads cabbage, shredded
5 green peppers, chopped
10 onions, chopped
2 cans chopped pimento
4 c. corn oil
8 c. vinegar
9 c. sugar
4 c. honey
8 tsp. salt

Mix cabbage, green peppers, onions and pimento in large bowl. Combine oil, vinegar, sugar, honey and salt in large saucepan. Cook until thickened, stirring frequently. Pour over vegetables; mix gently. Store, covered, in refrigerator for 3 to 4 days. Yield: 100 servings.

Hazel Brown
Indianapolis, IN

Nine-Day Slaw

1 med. cabbage, grated
2 stalks celery, chopped
2 med. onions, chopped
1 green pepper, chopped
2 c. sugar
½ c. oil
½ c. cider vinegar
1 tbsp. sugar
1 tbsp. salt
Chopped pimento (opt.)

Combine vegetables and 2 cups sugar in bowl; mix well. Mix remaining ingredients in small bowl. Pour over vegetables. Chill, covered, for 1 to 9 days. Yield: 12-15 servings.

Lois H. Webber
East Forsyth H.S., Kernersville, NC

Apple-Carrot Salad

2 c. shredded carrots
1½ c. chopped unpeeled apple
½ c. raisins
¼ c. chopped walnuts
½ c. mayonnaise
1 tbsp. lemon juice
1 tbsp. honey

Combine carrots, apple, raisins and walnuts in bowl. Mix remaining ingredients in small bowl. Pour over salad; toss to coat well. Chill, covered, for 2 to 3 hours. Spoon onto lettuce-lined salad plates. Garnish with coconut if desired. Yield: 12 servings.

Juanita Boyce
Lawton H.S., Lawton, OK

Marinated Carrots

3 lb. carrots, peeled, sliced
2 sm. onions, thinly sliced
1 green pepper, thinly sliced
1 c. vinegar
½ c. oil
1 c. sugar
1 tbsp. Worcestershire sauce
1 tsp. prepared mustard

Cook carrots in a small amount of water in saucepan until tender. Drain and cool. Combine with onions and green pepper in bowl. Mix vinegar, oil, sugar, Worcerstershire sauce and mustard in small bowl. Pour over carrot mixture. Chill, covered, for 24 hours or longer. Yield: 12 servings.

Jean Holbrook
Supervisor of H.E., Roanoke Co. Sch., Salem, VA

Cucumber and Onion Salad

8 lb. cucumbers, peeled
2½ lb. onions
1 qt. cider vinegar
2 c. oil
2 c. cold water
2 tbsp. sugar
2 tbsp. salt
2 tsp. pepper
4 heads leaf lettuce, separated

Slice cucumbers and onons very thin. Combine in bowl. Mix vinegar, oil, water, sugar and seasonings in bowl. Pour over cucumber mixture; mix well. Chill for 1 hour. Place lettuce leaves on salad plates. Drain cucumber mixture. Spoon onto lettuce leaves. Garnish with parsley. Yield: 50 servings.

Kathy Thomas
Chickasha Mid. Sch., Chickasha, OK

DeOlivi Salad

1 c. chopped celery
1 c. sliced carrots
1 c. sliced black olives
1 c. sliced green olives
1   8-oz. bottle of Golden Blend
*   Italian dressing*

Combine celery, carrots and olives in salad bowl. Add dressing; mix well. Marinate in refrigerator until serving time. Yield: 12 servings.
Note: May add chopped vegetables such as zucchini, peppers, broccoli or cauliflower.

Nancy Doughty
Newcastle H.S., Newcastle, OK

Layered Green Salad

1 head red leaf lettuce, torn
1 head iceberg lettuce, torn
½ pkg. fresh spinach, torn
1 can small green peas
6 hard-boiled eggs, chopped
½ c. bacon bits
2 bunches green onions, chopped
1 lg. carton sour cream
2 c. mayonnaise
2 pkg. ranch-style dressing mix

Layer leaf lettuce, iceberg lettuce, spinach, peas, eggs, bacon bits and green onions in clear glass bowl. Mix remaining ingredients in small bowl. Spread over salad, sealing to side of bowl. Chill for 24 hours. Yield: 12 servings.

Doretha C. Gilmore
Azalia Mid. Sch., Mobile, AL

Potato Salad

15 med. potatoes, peeled, chopped
2 tsp. salt
½ c. finely chopped onion
Salt and pepper to taste
½ c. Italian dressing
1 c. mayonnaise
⅓ c. mustard
2 c. chopped celery
4 hard-boiled eggs, chopped
½ c. pickle relish

Bring enough water to cover potatoes to a boil in saucepan. Add potatoes and 2 teaspoons salt. Cook, covered, for 30 minutes or until tender. Drain and cool. Combine with onion in bowl. Sprinkle with salt and pepper to taste. Add Italian dressing; mix well. Chill, covered, for 2 hours or longer. Add remaining ingredients; mix lightly. Yield: 15 servings.

Nancy B. Womack
Botetourt Vo. Sch., Fincastle, VA

Reunion Potato Salad

5 lb. potatoes
8 hard-boiled eggs
1 c. chopped green onions
2 c. thinly sliced celery
1 10-oz. jar dill pickle relish
1 c. mayonnaise
1 c. salad dressing
1 tsp. celery seed
1½ tsp. salt
½ tsp. pepper

Cook potatoes in skins in water to cover in saucepan until tender. Drain potatoes and remove skins. Put potatoes and eggs through food chopper. Combine with green onions, celery and relish in bowl. Mix remaining ingredients in small bowl. Add half the dressing to salad; toss to coat well. Chill, covered, in refrigerator. Add remaining dressing; mix well. Chill, covered, for several hours to overnight. Yield: 24 servings.

Jayne Garber
East Clinton H.S., Sabina, OH

Italian Vegetable Toss

1 6-oz. can artichoke hearts
1½ c. shell macaroni, cooked
2 c. broccoli flowerets
1 c. cauliflowerets
1 c. sliced ripe olives
1 c. sliced fresh mushrooms
½ c. chopped green onions
⅔ c. Italian dressing
1 med. avocado, sliced
1 med. tomato, chopped

Rinse and chop artichoke hearts. Combine with macaroni, broccoli flowerets, cauliflowerets, olives, mushrooms and green onions in bowl. Add Italian dressing; toss to mix well. Chill, covered, for several hours. Add avocado and tomato at serving time; toss gently. Yield: 12-16 servings.

Ann McMullin
Smith Cotton H.S., Sedalia, MO

Zesty Vegetable Salad

1 16-oz. can cut green beans, drained
1 16-oz. can kidney beans, drained
1 7-oz. can pitted ripe olives, drained
1 15-oz. jar marinated artichoke hearts, drained
1½ c. diagonally sliced celery
1 med. red onion, thinly sliced
1 6 to 8-oz. can mushrooms, drained
1 4-oz. jar chopped pimento, drained
¼ c. tarragon vinegar
½ c. oil or artichoke marinade
¼ tsp. Tabasco sauce
1 tsp. sugar
1¼ tsp. salt

Combine green beans, kidney beans, olives, artichoke hearts, celery, onion, mushrooms and pimento in large bowl; mix gently. Combine tarragon vinegar, oil, Tabasco sauce, sugar and salt in jar; shake well. Pour over vegetables; toss gently to coat. Chill, covered, overnight. Garnish with parsley. Yield: 15 servings.

Susan R. Barrow
Layton, UT

Marinade for Vegetable Salad

1½ c. wine vinegar
¾ c. oil
⅓ c. sugar
2 cloves of garlic, minced
2 tsp. prepared mustard
1 tbsp. oregano
2 tbsp. salt
Pepper to taste

Combine vinegar, oil, sugar, garlic, mustard, oregano, salt and pepper to taste in bowl; mix well. Pour over chopped fresh vegetables such as zucchini, mushrooms, broccoli and cauliflower. Chill overnight. Yield: 2½ cups.

Pat Vaughan
Fairfield Comm. H.S., Fairfield, IL

Marinated Vegetables

¾ c. vinegar
½ c. oil
1 c. sugar
1 tsp. each salt, pepper
1 can French-style green beans
  with red pepper
1 can green peas
1 can Shoe Peg corn
1 can whole kernel corn
1 sm. jar pimento
1 green pepper, chopped
1 c. each chopped onion, celery
¾ c. chopped carrot (opt.)

Bring vinegar, oil, sugar, salt and pepper to a boil in saucepan. Drain canned vegetables and pimento. Combine with green pepper, onion, celery and carrot in bowl. Add dressing; mix well. Chill, covered, for 8 hours to 2 weeks. Yield: 12-15 servings.

Katherine Anderson
East Central H.S., Lucedale, MS

Shrimp Salad

6 chicken breasts
3 lb. shrimp, cooked
4 pkg. imitation crab meat
3 cans pineapple tidbits, drained
5 c. seedless green grapes
4 c. chopped celery
Thinly sliced almonds
¼ c. sugar
1½ tbsp. flour
½ tsp. salt
1 egg
2 tbsp. vinegar
¾ c. pineapple juice

Cook chicken in salted water to cover in saucepan until tender. Drain and chop into bite-sized pieces. Combine with shrimp, crab meat, pineapple, grapes, celery and almonds in large bowl; mix well. Blend remaining ingredients in saucepan. Cook until thickened, stirring constantly. Cool. Add to shrimp mixture; mix lightly. Chill until serving time. Yield: 15 servings.

Beverley C. Goodman
Smyth Co. Vo. Sch., Marion, VA

Tomatoes Stuffed with Shrimp and Peas

1 c. each mayonnaise, sour cream
4 tsp. tarragon vinegar
4 tsp. Dijon mustard
2 tsp. dillweed
2 tsp. salt
3 10-oz. packages frozen green peas
1½ lb. small shrimp, cooked
8 hard-boiled eggs, chopped
1 c. sweet pickle relish
4 stalks celery, chopped
20 med. tomatoes

Blend mayonnaise, sour cream, vinegar, mustard, dillweed and 2 teaspoons salt in large bowl. Rinse peas in cold water; drain. Add to dressing with shrimp, eggs, relish and celery; toss to coat evenly. Chill, covered, for 2 hours. Remove tomato stems and cut each into 6 wedges, cutting to but not through bottom. Place on lettuce-lined plates, separating wedges slightly. Stuff with shrimp mixture. Yield: 20 servings.

Jackie Grantham
Valdosta, GA

Taco Salad

2 lb. ground beef
1 c. catsup
2½ tsp. (or more) chili powder
2 tsp. oregano
¼ tsp. each salt and pepper
2 lg. heads lettuce, torn
4 tomatoes, chopped
2½ c. grated cheese
2 6-oz. cans pitted ripe olives
1 c. mayonnaise
1 c. (or more) taco sauce
2 10-oz. packages regular corn chips,
  broken

Brown ground beef in 10-inch skillet, stirring until crumbly; drain. Stir in next 5 ingredients. Simmer for several minutes. Cool. Combine lettuce, tomatoes, cheese and olives in bowl. Add ground beef mixture. Mix mayonnaise and taco sauce in bowl. Add to salad; toss lightly. Add corn chips just before serving; mix lightly. Yield: 14 servings.

Ann Hodgson
Dodgeland H.S., Juneau, WI

Frog-Eye Salad

1 c. sugar
2 tbsp. flour
½ tsp. salt
1¾ c. pineapple juice
2 eggs, beaten
1 tbsp. lemon juice
3 qt. water
1 tbsp. oil
2 tsp. salt
1 16-oz. package acini-de-pepe pasta
3 11-oz. cans mandarin oranges,
  drained
2 20-oz. cans pineapple chunks, drained
1 20-oz. can crushed pineapple, drained
1 13-oz. carton whipped topping
1 c. miniature marshmallows
1 c. coconut

Mix sugar, flour and ½ teaspoon salt in saucepan. Blend in pineapple juice and eggs gradually. Cook over medium heat until thickened, stirring constantly. Stir in lemon juice. Cool to room temperature. Bring water, oil and 2 teaspoons salt to a boil in saucepan. Add pasta. Cook until tender; drain and rinse. Combine with cooled sauce in bowl; mix lightly. Chill, well covered, overnight. Add remaining ingredients; mix well. Chill, covered, until serving time. Yield: 30 servings.

Judy Meek
Marshall Jr. H.S., Wichita, KS

Macaroni Salad

1 8-oz. package macaroni
1 8-oz. bottle of Italian dressing
1 c. chopped celery
¾ c. shredded carrots
¾ c. chopped green pepper
¼ c. chopped onion
½ c. chopped cheese
1 8-oz. carton sour cream

Cook macaroni according to package directions; drain. Mix with Italian dressing in bowl. Chill, covered, overnight. Add vegetables and cheese; mix well. Fold in sour cream. Yield: 15 servings.

Jean Holbrook
Supervisor of H.E., Roanoke Co. Sch., Salem, VA

Summer Macaroni Salad

1 16-oz. package spiral macaroni
5 oz. frozen peas
3 hard-boiled eggs, chopped
½ c. chopped sweet pickles
½ c. chopped celery
1 med. onion, chopped
1 c. cubed Cheddar cheese
2 c. mayonnaise
2 tsp. prepared mustard
⅓ c. Thousand Island dressing
1 tsp. celery seed
¼ c. sweet pickle juice
Salt and pepper to taste

Cook macaroni according to package directions, adding peas for last 3 to 4 minutes of cooking time; drain and rinse. Combine macaroni and peas with eggs, pickles, celery, onion and cheese in bowl; mix well. Mix mayonnaise, mustard, Thousand Island dressing, celery seed and pickle juice in bowl. Pour over salad; mix gently. Season with salt and pepper. Chill until serving time. Garnish with paprika. Yield: 12-15 servings.

Marla E. Franklin
Northeastern Jr.-Sr. H.S., Fountain City, IN

Pepper Dressing

1 qt. mayonnaise
1 c. water
1 tbsp. lemon juice
2 dashes Tabasco sauce
1 tsp. Worcestershire sauce
1 tsp. steak sauce
¼ c. Parmesan cheese
1½ tsp. dry mustard
1½ tsp. garlic powder
1½ tsp. sugar
1 tbsp. salt
2 tbsp. coarsely ground black pepper

Combine all ingredients in large bowl. Blend well with wire whisk. Store, covered, in refrigerator for 24 hours or longer. Yield: 5 cups.

Ann W. Jackson
Bedford Ed. Center, Bedford, VA

MAIN DISHES

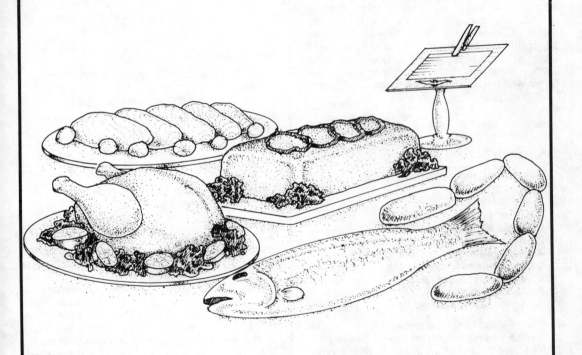

Barbecue Beef

    1   3 to 4-lb. boneless round roast
    2 tbsp. oil
    1 lg. onion, thinly sliced
    1 clove of garlic, minced
    1   18-oz. jar barbecue sauce
    ½ c. water
    ¼ tsp. liquid smoke (opt.)
    2 tbsp. brown sugar
    3 tbsp. flour
    ¾ c. cold water

Brown roast in oil in pressure cooker. Remove roast to platter. Sauté onion and garlic in pan drippings. Stir in barbecue sauce, ½ cup water and liquid smoke. Place roast on rack in pressure cooker. Cook at 15 pounds pressure for 40 minutes. Remove cooker from heat; allow pressure to drop. Remove roast to serving platter. Remove rack from cooker. Stir brown sugar into sauce. Blend flour and ¾ cup cold water in small bowl. Add to sauce. Cook over medium heat until thickened, stirring constantly. Serve with roast. Yield: 12 servings.

Linda Wright
Idabel H.S., Foreman, AR

Stroganoff For-A-Crowd

    8 lb. round steak, partially frozen
    ¼ c. shortening
    ¼ tsp. pepper
    2 c. chopped onion
    2 cloves of garlic, minced
    2   6-oz. cans sliced mushrooms
    4 cans cream of mushroom soup
    1 can condensed beef broth
    1   6-oz. can tomato paste
    3 c. sour cream
    18 oz. noodles, cooked

Cut steak into ½ x 2-inch strips. Brown 1 pound at a time in shortening in heavy saucepan. Return beef to saucepan. Sprinkle with pepper. Add onion, garlic and mushrooms. Blend soup, broth and tomato paste in bowl. Stir into beef mixture. Simmer, covered, for 1¼ hours or until tender, stirring occasionally. Stir a small amount of hot mixture into sour cream; stir sour cream into hot mixture. Cook just until heated through. Serve over hot noodles. Yield: 24 servings.

Dollie Edwards
Claxton H.S., Claxton, GA

Sweet and Sour Roast

    5 onions, thinly sliced
    ¼ c. butter
    1 tsp. salt
    3 c. boiling water
    1   4 to 5-lb. boneless chuck roast
    3 tbsp. brown sugar
    ¼ c. lemon juice

Sauté onions in butter in heavy saucepan. Stir in salt and water. Place roast in saucepan. Simmer for 2 hours or until tender. Remove roast to warm platter; slice thinly. Stir brown sugar and lemon juice into pan juices. Add roast slices. Simmer for 30 minutes longer. Spoon over French bread. Yield: 12-15 servings.

Dorothy Moore
Central Jr. H.S., Sand Springs, OK

Swiss Steak

    48 lb. round steak, sliced ¾ inch thick
    6 c. flour
    6 c. (about 2 lb.) shortening
    3 c. flour
    3 qt. water
    12 c. chopped celery
    12 c. chopped green pepper
    12   28-oz. cans tomatoes
    ½ c. salt
    2 tbsp. pepper
    24 bay leaves

Cut round steak into 100 serving pieces. Dredge in 6 cups flour, coating well. Reserve remaining flour. Brown steak in shortening in large skillet. Remove to shallow baking pan. Blend 3 cups flour and reserved flour into pan drippings. Combine flour paste with remaining ingredients in stockpot. Cook over medium heat until thickened, stirring constantly. Pour over steak. Bake, covered, at 325 degrees for 2½ to 3 hours or until steak is tender. May remove cover during last 30 minutes of baking time if desired. Remove bay leaves. Yield: 100 servings.

Marlene Hoenig
Tupelo, MS

Barbecue

20 lb. ground beef
6 lg. onions, chopped
2 bunches celery, chopped
1   No. 10 can catsup
¼ c. packed brown sugar
¼ c. each vinegar, barbecue sauce
1 c. lemon juice
¼ c. Worcestershire sauce
2 tbsp. prepared mustard
2 cloves of garlic, chopped
2 tbsp. each salt and pepper

Crumble ground beef into large roaster. Bake at 325 degrees for 45 minutes, stirring every 15 minutes. Mix in remaining ingredients. Bake for 30 minutes longer. Yield: 30-40 servings.

Judy Murray
Lake Mills H.S., Lake Mills, WI

Party Barbecues

20 lb. ground beef
2 c. butter
2 c. minced onion
5 c. chopped celery
1   No. 10 can tomato catsup
2 c. sugar
1 c. vinegar
¼ c. mustard
Salt to taste

Brown ground beef in butter in electric roaster, stirring until crumbly. Add remaining ingredients; mix well. Cook at 125 to 150 degrees for 1 hour or to desired consistency. Serve over hamburger buns if desired. Yield: 100 servings.

Bobbie D. Smith
Waynoka H.S., Waynoka, OK

Mom's Chili Beans

2 lb. dried beans
2 tbsp. salt
2 lb. ground beef
2 lg. onions, chopped
4 cloves of garlic, chopped
1 can tomatoes, chopped
1   4-oz. can green chilies
1   8-oz. jar taco sauce
2 tbsp. chili powder
½ tsp. cumin
1½ tsp. pepper

Soak beans in water to cover in saucepan overnight; drain and rinse. Add salt and fresh water to cover. Cook for 1 hour. Brown ground beef in skillet, stirring until crumbly; drain. Add ground beef and remaining ingredients to beans; mix well. Simmer for 1½ hours, stirring occasionally and adding water if necessary to make of desired consistency. Yield: 12 servings.

Shari Rogers
Lincoln Mid. Sch., Abilene, TX

Church Supper Casserole

3 lb. ground beef
1 c. chopped onion
2   12-oz. cans whole kernel corn, drained
6 c. cooked noodles
2 cans Cheddar cheese soup
2 c. sour cream
½ c. chopped pimento
1 tsp. each salt and pepper
2 c. cracker crumbs
1 c. shredded Cheddar cheese
½ c. (or less) melted margarine

Brown ground beef in skillet, stirring until crumbly. Add onion. Sauté until tender; drain. Mix in next 7 ingredients.. Spoon into greased 9 x 13-inch baking dish. Sprinkle with cracker crumbs and cheese. Dot with butter. Bake at 350 degrees for 45 minutes. Yield: 12-15 servings.

Emily Lewis
Capitol Hill H.S., Oklahoma City, OK

Basic Meatballs

5 lb. ground beef
⅔ c. fine dry bread crumbs
3 tbsp. minced onion
3 eggs, slightly beaten
2½ tsp. salt
½ tsp. pepper

Combine ground beef with remaining ingredients in bowl; mix well. Shape into 1-inch balls. Place on baking sheet. Bake at 350 degrees for 25 to 30 minutes; drain. Add to favorite spaghetti sauce or other recipe using meatballs.
Yield: 25 servings.

Cinda Stocks
Blue Mound H.S., Blue Mound, IL

Creamed Tacos

 2 lb. ground beef
 1 lb. brick chili
 1 can Ro-Tel tomatoes
 1 lb. Velveeta cheese, chopped
 1 can chili beans
 ½ pt. whipping cream
 12 to 16 oz. nacho cheese taco chips
 10 oz. Cheddar cheese, grated
 ⅓ to ½ head lettuce, chopped
 2 med. tomatoes, chopped
 ½ onion, chopped

Brown ground beef in skillet, stirring until crumbly; drain. Season to taste. Combine with chili, Ro-Tel tomatoes, Velveeta cheese, beans and cream in large Crock•Pot. Cook on Low for several hours or to desired consistency, stirring occasionally. Place remaining ingredients in individual serving bowls. Allow diners to serve themselves by layering chips, ground beef mixture and remaining ingredients on plates. Yield: 12-14 servings.

Trudy K. Miller
Bishop Carroll H.S., Wichita, KS

Ground Beef-Noodle Bake

 4 lb. ground beef
 3 c. chopped onions
 1 c. chopped green pepper
 3 to 4 lb. noodles
 3 cans tomato soup
 12 oz. chili sauce
 ¼ c. chopped pimento
 4 c. shredded American cheese
 2 tsp. salt
 ½ tsp. pepper
 2 c. water
 4½ c. bread crumbs
 ¼ c. melted butter

Brown ground beef, onion and green pepper in skillet, stirring frequently; drain. Cook noodles according to package directions; drain. Add ground beef mixture, soup, chili sauce, pimento, cheese, salt and pepper; mix well. Stir in water. Spoon into two 9x13-inch baking dishes. Toss crumbs with butter in bowl. Sprinkle over top. Bake at 350 degrees for 45 minutes. Garnish with green pepper rings. Yield: 24 servings.

Ann H. Brown
Christian Co. H.S., Hopkinsville, KY

Lasagna

 1½ lb. ground beef
 1 16-oz. can tomatoes
 1 12-oz. can tomato paste
 1 tbsp. basil
 ¼ tsp. oregano
 1 tsp. each garlic salt, salt and pepper
 3 c. cottage cheese
 ¾ c. Parmesan cheese
 2 tbsp. parsley flakes
 2 eggs, beaten
 1 tsp. each salt and pepper
 10 oz. lasagna noodles, cooked
 16 oz. mozzarella cheese, sliced

Brown ground beef in skillet, stirring until crumbly; drain. Add next 7 ingredients; mix well. Simmer for 30 minutes, stirring occasionally. Combine cottage cheese, Parmesan cheese, parsley flakes, eggs, 1 teaspoon salt and 1 teaspoon pepper in bowl; mix well. Layer noodles, cottage cheese mixture, mozzarella cheese and sauce ½ at a time in 9x13-inch baking dish. Bake at 375 degrees for 30 minutes. Cool for 10 minutes before serving. Yield: 12 servings.

Patricia M. Todd
Western Branch H.S., Suffolk, VA

Lasagna for Sixteen

 3 lb. ground beef
 1 med. onion, minced
 1 clove of garlic, minced
 1 tsp. minced parsley
 1½ 6-oz. cans tomato paste
 2 16-oz. jars spaghetti sauce with
    mushrooms
 2 c. water
 ½ tsp. each salt and pepper
 2 tsp. MSG
 1 tbsp. oregano
 5 qt. water
 2 to 3 drops of olive oil
 16 oz. lasagna noodles
 16 oz. mozzarella cheese, thinly sliced
 12 oz. ricotta cheese
 2 tbsp. grated Romano cheese

Brown ground beef, onion, garlic and parsley in saucepan, stirring frequently; drain. Add next 7 ingredients; mix well. Simmer for 1½ to 2 hours. Bring 5 quarts water and olive oil to a boil in saucepan. Break noodles into halves; add to water. Cook for 20 minutes or until tender, stirring frequently; drain. Layer noodles, sauce, mozzarella cheese and ricotta cheese alternately in two 9x13-inch baking dishes until all ingredients are used. Sprinkle with Romano cheese. Bake at 375 degrees for 20 to 30 minutes or until bubbly. Yield: 16 servings.

Sharon Cooper
Chase H.S., Chase, KS

Lasagna for Twenty-Four

> 2 lb. ground beef
> ¼ c. chopped onion
> 2 env. spaghetti sauce mix
> 2   15-oz. cans tomato sauce
> 1 c. water
> 1   6-oz. can mushrooms, drained
> 16 oz. lasagna noodles, cooked
> 24 oz. cottage cheese
> 2 lb. mozzarella cheese, shredded

Brown ground beef and onion in skillet, stirring frequently; drain. Add spaghetti sauce mix, tomato sauce, water and mushrooms; mix well. Bring to a boil. Cook for 1 minute; reduce heat. Simmer for 10 minutes or to desired consistency. Layer noodles, sauce, cottage cheese and mozzarella cheese ⅓ at a time in lightly greased 11x17-inch baking pan. Bake at 350 degrees for 45 minutes. Let stand for 5 to 10 minutes before serving. Yield: 24 servings.

Carolyn Bailey
Shepherd Pub. Sch., Shepherd, MI

Quick And Easy Lasagna

> 2 lb. ground beef
> 2   32-oz. jars spaghetti sauce
> 2   12-oz. cans tomato juice
> 1 to 1½ lb. uncooked lasagna noodles
> 2 lb. mozzarella cheese, thinly sliced

Brown ground beef in saucepan, stirring until crumbly; drain. Stir in spaghetti sauce and tomato juice. Alternate layers of uncooked noodles, sauce and cheese ¼ at a time in each of 2 greased 9x13-inch baking dishes. Bake at 350 degrees for 1 hour. Yield: 12-16 servings.

Carla Seippel
Fort Osage Jr. H.S., Independence, MO

Mostaccioli

> 1 lb. ground beef
> 1 onion, chopped
> 1 green pepper, chopped
> 1   28-oz. can tomatoes
> 1   32-oz. jar spaghetti sauce
> 1 env. spaghetti sauce mix
> Salt, pepper, garlic salt and
>   Italian seasoning to taste
> 1   16-oz. package mostaccioli
> Several drops of oil
> 1 c. shredded mozzarella cheese

Brown ground beef and onion in skillet, stirring frequently; drain. Add next 8 ingredients; mix well. Simmer for 20 minutes. Cook pasta according to package directions, adding several drops of oil, just until tender; drain. Place on large platter. Spoon sauce over top. Sprinkle with cheese. Serve immediately.
Yield: 12 servings.

Barbara Tripp
Spring Lake Jr.-Sr. H.S., Spring Lake, MI

Italian Spaghetti

> 10 lb. ground beef
> ½ c. shortening
> ½ c. flour
> 32 oz. each tomato paste, tomato sauce
> 2 gal. water
> 10 med. onions, chopped
> 1¼ c. each chopped green pepper, celery
> 40 bay leaves
> ½ c. chili powder
> 3 tbsp. each oregano, basil and thyme
> ⅓ c. salt
> 3 tbsp. pepper
> 7 lb. spaghetti, cooked

Brown ground beef in shortening in large stockpot, stirring until crumbly; drain. Sprinkle flour over ground beef. Add remaining ingredients; mix well. Simmer for 3 to 4 hours or to desired consistency. Remove bay leaves. Serve over hot spaghetti. Yield: 50 servings.

Eula Mae Dyar
Puckett H.S., Mendenhall, MS

Kids' Favorite Spaghetti Sauce

11½ lb. ground beef
2 tsp. garlic powder
5 lg. onions, chopped
12 15-oz. cans tomato sauce
6 12-oz. cans tomato paste
⅓ c. sugar
6 tbsp. parsley flakes
2 tbsp. oregano
¼ c. basil
2 tbsp. salt
1 tbsp. pepper
4 c. water
¾ c. flour
8 lb. spaghetti, cooked

Brown ground beef in 5-gallon stockpot, stirring until crumbly; drain. Add garlic powder and onions. Sauté until onions are transparent. Add tomato sauce, tomato paste, sugar and seasonings; mix well. Simmer for 2 hours, stirring occasionally. Blend water and flour in bowl. Stir into sauce. Cook until thickened, stirring constantly. Serve over hot spaghetti.
Yield: 65 servings.

Cindy Josephson
Johnson-Brock H.S., Johnson, NE

Spaghetti Pie

12 oz. spaghetti, cooked
¼ c. butter
1 c. grated Cheddar cheese
4 eggs, beaten
2 c. cottage cheese
2 lb. ground beef
1 c. chopped onion
½ c. chopped green pepper
16 oz. tomatoes, chopped
2 6-oz. cans tomato paste
1 tbsp. sugar
1 tbsp. oregano
1 tsp. garlic salt
1 c. grated mozzarella cheese

Drain hot spaghetti. Stir in butter, Cheddar cheese and eggs; mix well. Spread in two 9x13-inch baking dishes. Spread cottage cheese over spaghetti. Brown ground beef with onion and green pepper in skillet, stirring frequently; drain. Add tomatoes, tomato paste, sugar, oregano and garlic salt; mix well. Spoon into prepared dishes. Bake at 325 degrees for 25 to 30 minutes. Sprinkle with mozzarella cheese. Bake for 5 minutes longer. Yield: 12 servings.
Note: May be prepared ahead and frozen. Reheat at 325 degrees.

Marian E. Baker
Sycamore H.S., Sycamore, IL

Spaghetti Sauce

2 to 2½ lb. lean ground chuck
2 lg. onions, chopped
2 c. fresh mushrooms
2 32-oz. jars spaghetti sauce
2 oz. tomato paste
2 tbsp. sugar
2 tsp. crushed red pepper
Salt, garlic powder, oregano and
*   thyme to taste*

Brown chuck in heavy saucepan, stirring until crumbly; drain. Add remaining ingredients; mix well. Simmer for 1½ to 3 hours. Serve over hot pasta with Parmesan cheese.
Yield: 12-15 servings.
Note: May substitute ground turkey. Sauce may be reheated but red pepper will intensify.

Debra Greenwood
Clinton Jr. H.S., Knoxville, TN

Upside-Down Ground Beef Pie

3 lb. ground beef
2¼ c. chopped onion
2¼ c. chopped celery
¾ c. chopped green pepper
3 cans tomato soup
1 tbsp. Worcestershire sauce
1½ tsp. salt
6 c. flour
3 tbsp. baking powder
1½ tsp. soda
2 tsp. salt
1 c. shortening
2 to 3 c. buttermilk

Brown ground beef in large saucepan; drain. Add onion, celery and green pepper. Cook over medium heat for 5 minutes. Stir in soup, Worcestershire sauce and 1½ teaspoons salt. Heat just to the boiling point. Spoon into three 8-inch iron skillets. Combine flour and remaining dry ingredients in bowl. Cut in shortening until crumbly. Add enough buttermilk to make soft dough, mixing just until dry ingredients are moistened. Knead 8 to 10 times on lightly floured surface; divide into 3 portions. Roll each portion into 8-inch circle. Place over ground beef mixture. Bake at 450 degrees for 15 minutes. Yield: 18 servings.

Note: May omit soda and substitute sweet milk for buttermilk.

Shirley Henkel
Statesville H.S., Statesville, NC

Grandma D's Pierogi

1 to 1½ lb. ground beef
1 egg, beaten
2 tbsp. bread crumbs
1 onion, finely chopped
Salt, pepper and garlic powder to taste
2 c. flour
½ tsp. salt
1 egg
Chopped parsley
Chopped onion
Bacon drippings

Combine ground beef, 1 egg, bread crumbs and 1 onion in bowl. Add salt, pepper and garlic powder to taste; mix well. Mix flour and ½ teaspoon salt in bowl. Add 1 egg and enough lukewarm water to make easy to handle dough. Roll into ⅛-inch thick rectangle on floured surface. Cut into 3-inch squares. Place 1 tablespoon ground beef mixture on each square. Fold over to enclose filling; seal edges well. Place in boiling water in saucepan. Cook for 15 to 20 minutes; drain well. Sauté pierogi in parsley and onion to taste in a small amount of bacon drippings in skillet. Place in serving bowl. Garnish with bacon bits. Yield: 12 servings.

Carol DeReu
Forest View H.S., Wheeling, IL

Chalupas

1   13-lb. pork roast
1½ lb. dried pinto beans
2 cloves of garlic, chopped
1 sm. can chopped green chilies, drained
2 tbsp. chili powder
1 tbsp. cumin
1 tsp. oregano
Salt to taste
Corn chips
Shredded Cheddar cheese
Shredded lettuce
Chopped tomatoes
Chopped onion
Taco sauce

Place roast in large heavy saucepan. Add beans, garlic, green chilies, seasonings and water to cover. Cook over medium heat until roast and beans are tender, adding water as necessary. Remove roast to platter; cool slightly. Shred into bite-sized pieces. Stir into beans. Cook, uncovered, until of desired consistency. Serve over corn chips; top with remaining ingredients. Yield: 12 servings.

Nancy Cantwell
Stewart Jr. H.S., Oxford, OH

Rio Grande Pork Roast

1   3 to 5-lb. boneless pork roast
½ tsp. chili powder
½ tsp. garlic salt
½ tsp. salt
¾ c. apple jelly
½ c. catsup
1 tbsp. vinegar
½ tsp. chili powder
1 c. crushed corn chips

Rub roast with mixture of ½ teaspoon chili powder, garlic salt and salt. Place on rack in roasting pan. Bake at 325 degrees for 45 to 55 minutes. Let stand for 15 minutes. Slice roast thinly; arrange slices in shallow baking dish. Combine jelly, catsup, vinegar and ½ teaspoon chili powder in saucepan. Bring to a boil; mix well. Simmer for 15 minutes. Pour over pork. Top with corn chips. Bake for 20 to 30 minutes longer. Yield: 12-16 servings.

Tamara Friesen
Jardine Jr. H.S., Wichita, KS

Junk Fried Rice

2 tbsp. oil
1 clove of garlic, sliced
½ tsp. crushed chili peppers
1½ c. chopped cooked lean pork
2 tbsp. oil
1 clove of garlic, sliced
½ tsp. crushed chili peppers
1 c. ½-inch green onion pieces
½ c. chopped sweet red pepper
½ c. chopped green pepper
1   8-oz. can water chestnuts, chopped
1 c. sliced mushrooms
1   2-oz. jar pimentos
1½ tbsp. oil
3 c. cooked rice, chilled
¼ c. light soy sauce
1 tbsp. Sake or Sherry
½ tsp. sugar
1 egg, beaten

Pour 2 tablespoons oil into preheated wok; swirl to coat well. Add 1 clove of garlic and ½ teaspoon chili peppers. Stir-fry until brown. Remove with slotted spoon and discard. Add pork. Stir-fry for 1 minute. Remove to drain on paper towel. Add 2 tablespoons oil, 1 clove of garlic and ½ teaspoon chili peppers. Stir-fry until brown. Remove with slotted spoon and discard. Add green onions, red and green pepper, water chestnuts, mushrooms and pimentos. Stir-fry for 2 to 3 minutes. Remove to drain on paper towels. Add 1½ tablespoons oil and rice. Stir-fry for 2 mintues. Stir in stir-fried vegetables and pork. Mix soy sauce, wine and sugar in small bowl. Add to wok; mix well. Make a well in center. Pour egg into well. Cook for 30 seconds or just until egg begins to set, stirring egg with chopstick. Toss egg with rice mixture for 30 seconds.
Yield: 12 servings.
Note: Rice should be chilled for 2 days to prevent stickiness. May substitute chicken, ham or shrimp for pork.

Annie Rust
Blanchard H.S., Norman, OK

Country-Style Ribs

1 sm. onion, chopped
2 sticks butter
1 c. vinegar
1½ c. packed brown sugar
2   28-oz. bottles hickory smoke-flavored barbecue sauce
½ c. catsup
2 tsp. Worcestershire sauce
2 tbsp. mustard
2 dashes of liquid smoke
Pepper to taste
12 lb. country-style ribs

Sauté onion in butter in saucepan. Add remaining ingredients except ribs; mix well. Cook over medium heat for several minutes, stirring occasionally. Combine ribs with salted water to cover and 1 cup sauce in 12-quart stockpot. Cook for 2 hours. Drain. Place ribs on grill. Baste with sauce. Grill until brown and tender. Serve with remaining sauce.

Annie Rust
Blanchard H.S., Norman, OK

Ham and Asparagus Mornay

200 cooked asparagus spears
100   ⅛-inch thick ham slices
1 gal. milk
5 sticks butter
5 c. flour
12 egg yolks
½ c. light cream
Salt to taste
6 oz. Parmesan cheese
2 sticks butter, sliced

Place 2 asparagus spears on each ham slice. Roll up to enclose asparagus. Arrange in large baking pan. Heat milk in saucepan. Melt 5 sticks butter in large saucepan. Blend in flour. Cook over low heat for 5 minutes, stirring constantly. Stir in hot milk gradually. Cook until thickened, stirring constantly. Beat egg yolks and cream in bowl. Stir a small amount of hot mixture into egg yolk mixture; stir egg yolks into hot mixture. Add salt. Cook for 1 minute; remove from heat. Stir in Parmesan cheese. Pour over ham rolls. Dot with sliced butter. Sprinkle with paprika. Bake at 350 degrees for 30 minutes or until bubbly.
Yield: 50 servings.

Ann W. Jackson
Bedford Ed. Center, Bedford, VA

Barbecue Sauce for Chicken

1 qt. white vinegar
1 c. shortening
1 stick butter
¼ box red pepper
2¼ tsp. pepper
1 tbsp. salt

Combine all ingredients in saucepan. Heat until shortening is melted; mix well. Dip chicken halves into sauce; place on grill. Brush generously and frequently with sauce while cooking. Yield: 5-6 cups.

Nora Sweat
West Hardin H.S., Elizabethtown, KY

Broiled Lemon Chicken

6 lb. chicken breasts
¼ c. oil
½ c. soy sauce
Juice of 2 lemons
4 cloves of garlic, minced
2 tsp. salt
½ tsp. white pepper

Soak wooden skewers in water. Bone chicken and cut into pieces. Combine remaining ingredients in bowl; mix well. Add chicken; coat well. Marinate in refrigerator for 2 hours or longer. Drain, reserving marinade. Thread chicken onto prepared skewers. Brush with reserved marinade. Broil or grill 6 inches from heat source until tender, basting with reserved marinade occasionally. Serve with Creamy Lemon Rice (page 67). Yield: 12 servings.

Jane Bigler
Hillcrest Jr. H.S., Lenexa, KS

Chicken Breasts Oriental

1 lb. butter
50 chicken breasts
3 tbsp. salt
1 c. melted butter
3   6-oz. cans frozen orange juice
*   concentrate*
2 c. orange marmalade
Sugar to taste
½ c. soy sauce
1 tsp. ginger
26 c. cooked rice

Melt 1 pound butter in saucepan. Divide between three 13x19-inch baking pans. Wash chicken and pat dry. Arrange in prepared pans. Sprinkle with salt. Bake at 425 degrees until browned, turning once. Combine 1 cup melted butter, orange juice concentrate, marmalade, sugar, soy sauce and ginger in bowl; mix well. Add enough water to make of desired consistency. Brush over chicken. Bake at 350 degrees for 1 hour or until tender and well glazed. Serve with rice and garnish of avocado wedge on lettuce leaf. Yield: 50 servings.

Bobbie D. Smith
Waynoka H.S., Waynoka, OK

Imperial Chicken

1½ c. fine dry bread crumbs
1 c. Parmesan cheese
½ c. chopped fresh parsley
1 tsp. salt
½ tsp. pepper
1 c. melted butter
1 clove of garlic, minced
12 chicken breast filets
Juice of 2 lemons
Paprika

Mix first 5 ingredients in bowl. Combine melted butter and garlic. Dip filet into butter, then into crumb mixture. Roll into firm roll; secure with toothpicks. Arrange in foil-lined baking dish. Drizzle with lemon juice and remaining butter. Sprinkle with paprika. Bake at 350 degrees for 1 hour. Yield: 12 servings.

Janice Sapp
Claxton H.S., Claxton, GA

Chicken In Wine

12 chicken breasts, skinned
Seasoned salt to taste
3 cans mushroom soup
3 c. white wine

Rinse chicken; sprinkle with seasoned salt. Arrange in large baking dish. Combine soup and wine in blender container. Process until smooth. Pour over chicken. Bake at 350 degrees for 1½ hours, basting occasionally. Yield: 12 servings.

Jean Holbrook
Supervisor of H.E., Roanoke Co. Sch., Salem, VA

Quick and Easy Chicken Pie

8 chicken breasts
2 cans cream of chicken soup
2 c. self-rising flour
2 tsp. salt
1 tsp. pepper
2 c. buttermilk
2 sticks margarine, melted

Cook chicken in water to cover in large saucepan until tender. Drain, reserving 4 cups broth. Chop chicken; spread in large rectangular baking dish. Bring reserved broth and soup to a boil in saucepan. Pour over chicken. Combine flour and remaining ingredients in bowl; mix until smooth. Pour evenly over chicken. Bake at 425 degrees for 25 to 30 minutes or until brown.
Yield: 12 servings.

Vivian Pike
Bunker Hill H.S., Claremont, NC

Fruited Chicken

3 c. flour
1 tsp. each salt, garlic salt and celery salt
1 tsp. nutmeg
12 lb. chicken, cut up
1½ c. margarine
4   20-oz. cans pineapple tidbits
⅔ c. flour
¼ c. sugar
½ c. soy sauce

Combine 3 cups flour and seasonings in plastic bag. Add chicken several pieces at a time; shake to coat well. Brown chicken in margarine in skillet. Remove to 9x13-inch baking dishes, reserving pan drippings. Drain pineapple, reserving 2 cups juice. Spread pineapple over chicken. Stir ⅔ cup flour and sugar into reserved drippings in skillet. Add reserved pineapple juice and soy sauce. Cook until thickened, stirring constantly. Spoon over chicken. Bake, covered, at 350 degrees for 1 hour. Yield: 15 servings.

Hazel Jolliffe
Rolling Meadows H.S., Arlington Heights, IL

Kay's Favorite Chicken

12 chicken pieces
Garlic salt
Cornstarch
6 eggs, beaten
Oil
1½ c. rice vinegar
¾ c. chicken stock
3 tbsp. soy sauce
¾ tbsp. catsup
2½ c. sugar
1 tbsp. MSG (opt.)
1 tbsp. salt

Sprinkle chicken with garlic salt. Roll in cornstarch, coating well. Dip into eggs. Brown in a small amount of oil in skillet or electric skillet. Remove to large shallow baking dish. Combine remaining ingredients in saucepan. Bring to a boil; mix well. Pour over chicken. Bake at 350 degrees for 1 hour and 15 minutes.
Yield: 12 servings.
Note: May pour chicken stock mixture over browned chicken in skillet and simmer until chicken is tender.

Kay Caskey
Swope Mid. Sch., Reno, NV

Chicken Casserole

2 med. onions, finely chopped
1 stick margarine
4 cans cream of chicken soup
2 soup cans water
2 sm. cans chopped chili peppers
1 can sliced water chestnuts, drained
1 med. package tortilla chips
4 cans boned chicken
4 c. shredded Monterey Jack cheese

Satué onions in margarine in skillet. Add soup, water, chili peppers and water chestnuts; mix well. Layer chips, chicken, soup mixture and cheese in two 9x13-inch baking dishes. Bake at 350 degrees for 30 minutes.
Yield: 12-14 servings.

Kirby McHenry
Pascagoula H.S., Gautier, MS

Nacho Cheesecake

1¼ c. finely crushed tortilla chips
⅓ c. shredded longhorn cheese
¼ c. melted butter
3 med. ripe avocados
2 tbsp. lemon juice
24 oz. cream cheese, softened
5 eggs
¼ c. minced onion
10 dashes hot sauce
¼ tsp. garlic juice
1 tsp. Worcestershire sauce
1 tsp. salt
1½ c. chopped cooked chicken
1½ c. shredded longhorn cheese
½ c. shredded Monterey Jack cheese
    with jalapeños
16 oz. sour cream
2 tbsp. taco sauce
Chopped tomatoes
Minced green onions with tops

Combine tortilla chips, ⅓ cup longhorn cheese and butter in bowl; mix well. Press into bottom of 10-inch springform pan. Mash avocado with lemon juice in bowl. Add cream cheese; beat until smooth. Add eggs 1 at a time, beating well after each addition. Stir in onion, hot sauce, garlic juice, Worcestershire sauce and salt. Layer half the mixture, chicken, remaining cheeses and remaining cream cheese mixture in prepared pan. Bake at 350 degrees for 10 minutes. Reduce temperature to 250 degrees. Bake for 1 hour longer. Mix sour cream and taco sauce in bowl. Spread evenly over cheesecake. Bake at 350 degrees for 10 minutes. Cool completely on wire rack. Chill, covered, overnight or longer. Place on serving plate; remove side of pan. Sprinkle tomatoes in center of cheesecake. Sprinkle green onions in circle around tomatoes. Sprinkle ripe olives around outside edge. Serve with picante sauce and chili con queso dip. Yield: 12-16 servings.

Jane Bigler
Hillcrest Jr. H.S., Lenexa, KS

Javanese Dinner

5 c. warm cooked minute rice
1 lg. can chow mein noodles
2½ c. warm chopped cooked chicken
3 to 4 onions, minced
3 c. warm chicken gravy
2 c. chopped celery
1 lg. can crushed pineapple
2 c. warm chopped cooked chicken
3 c. warm chicken gravy
2 tomatoes, chopped
3 c. chopped American cheese
1 can cashews
1½ c. coconut
15 stemmed cherries

Place each ingredient in individual serving bowl. Arrange on buffet in order listed. Label each dish with flags numbered 1 through 14 on wooden sticks taped to the bowls. Place dinner plates by bowl number 1. Direct guests to layer ingredients in order on their dinner plates, beginning at bowl number 1. Yield: 15 servings.

Judy Murray
Lake Mills H.S., Lake Mills, WI

Scalloped Chicken

1 lb. chopped cooked chicken
1 qt. water
¼ c. shortening, melted
¼ c. flour
2 tsp. salt
1 c. milk, scalded
2 c. hot chicken broth
2 eggs, beaten
¾ lb. toasted bread cubes
2 c. hot chicken broth
Melted margarine to taste
1 egg, beaten
2 tsp. onion flakes
¼ c. chopped celery
¼ tsp. sage
2 tsp. salt
½ tsp. pepper

Simmer chicken in 1 quart water in saucepan for 5 minutes; drain. Blend shortening, flour and 2 teaspoons salt in saucepan. Stir in hot milk and 2 cups hot broth. Cook until thickened, stirring constantly. Stir a small amount of hot mixture into 2 eggs; stir eggs into hot mixture. Combine bread cubes and 2 cups hot broth in bowl. Add remaining ingredients; mix well. Layer dressing, half the sauce, chicken and remaining sauce in 10x15-inch baking pan. Bake at 350 degrees for 40 minutes. Yield: 12 servings.

Debra Hart
Emerson Jr. H.S., Enid, OK

Scalloped Chicken and Stuffing

 1 *8-oz. package herb stuffing mix*
 3 c. (or more) chopped cooked chicken
 ½ c. butter
 ½ c. flour
 ¼ tsp. salt
 Dash of pepper
 4 c. chicken broth
 6 eggs, slightly beaten
 1 can mushroom soup
 1 c. sour cream

Prepare stuffing mix according to package directions. Layer stuffing and chicken in 9x13-inch baking dish. Melt butter in saucepan. Blend in flour and seasonings. Stir in broth gradually. Cook until thickened, stirring constantly. Stir a small amount of hot mixture into eggs; stir eggs into hot mixture. Pour over layers. Bake at 350 degrees for 1 hour. Let stand for 5 minutes. Heat soup and sour cream to serving temperature in saucepan; mix well. Cut casserole into squares. Serve with hot mushroom sauce.
Yield: 12 servings.

Patricia Mikulecky
Bartlesville Mid. H.S., Bartlesville, OK

Easy Chicken Potpie

 1 stick margarine
 1 2½ to 3-lb. chicken, cooked, chopped
 1 can cream of celery soup
 2 15-oz. cans mixed vegetables, drained
 1½ c. chicken stock
 1½ c. buttermilk baking mix
 1½ c. milk

Melt margarine in rectangular baking dish; coat dish well. Pour off excess margarine and reserve. Combine chicken, soup, vegetables and stock in bowl; mix well. Spoon into prepared dish. Combine baking mix, milk and reserved margarine in bowl; mix just until moistened. Spread evenly over chicken. Bake at 350 degrees for 45 minutes to 1 hour.
Yield: 12 servings.

Dona McCload
Kempsville Jr. H.S., Virginia Beach, VA

Salmagundi

 1 2-in. bunch parsley
 2 2-oz. cans rolled anchovies with
 capers, drained
 8 oz. thinly sliced roast turkey
 8 oz. thinly sliced roast beef
 8 oz. feta cheese, cut into ½-in. cubes
 1 c. pitted ripe olives
 4 hard-boiled eggs, cut into quarters
 1 med. zucchini, thinly sliced
 30 to 40 cherry tomato halves
 ½ c. olive oil
 ⅓ c. red wine vinegar
 2 or 3 cloves of garlic, crushed
 ½ tsp. salt
 Freshly ground pepper

Trim stems from parsley. Place in center of 15-inch platter. Arrange anchovies in ring around parsley. Roll turkey and beef slices; cut into 2-inch pieces. Place turkey rolls in ring around anchovies. Alternate cheese cubes and olives in next circle. Arrange beef rolls, egg wedges, zucchini slices and cherry tomato halves in outer circle. Chill, covered, for 1 hour. Combine remaining ingredients in covered container; shake to mix well. Serve dressing and freshly ground pepper with salmagundi.
Yield: 12 servings.

Bobbie D. Smith
Waynoka H.S., Waynoka, OK

Holiday Turketti

 4 c. chopped cooked turkey
 12 oz. thin spaghetti, cooked
 1 lg. green pepper, minced
 1 med. onion, minced
 1 sm. jar pimento
 2 cans mushroom soup
 1½ c. broth
 ¼ tsp. celery salt
 ¼ tsp. pepper
 2 c. grated Cheddar cheese

Combine turkey with next 8 ingredients and 1½ cups cheese in bowl; mix well. Spoon into 3-quart baking dish. Chill overnight. Let stand until room temperature. Bake at 325 degrees for 1 hour. Sprinkle with remaining cheese. Garnish with parsley. Yield: 12 servings.

Doretha C. Gilmore
Azalea Mid. Sch., Mobile, AL

Crab Meat Burger

1   6 to 8-oz. can crab meat, drained
1 c. chopped celery
2 tbsp. grated onion
1 c. mayonnaise
6 English muffins, split
1 c. shredded medium sharp cheese

Combine crab meat, celery, onion and mayonnaise in bowl; mix well. Spread on English muffins. Sprinkle with cheese. Place on baking sheet. Broil for 2 to 3 minutes or until cheese is melted and brown on edges. Yield: 12 servings.

Polly Anne Bryant
Lonoke Jr. H.S., Lonoke, AR

Crab and Shrimp Casserole

2   6-oz. packages long grain and
     wild rice
6 tbsp. grated onion
1 c. chopped green pepper
1 c. chopped celery
¼ c. butter
2   6-oz. cans crab meat, drained, flaked
4   4-oz. cans shrimp, drained
2 cans cream of mushroom soup
1   4-oz. jar pimento, drained
2 tbsp. lemon juice

Prepare rice according to package directions. Sauté onion, green pepper and celery in butter in saucepan for 5 to 6 minutes. Stir in rice and remaining ingredients. Spoon into 4-quart baking dish. Bake at 325 degrees for 45 minutes to 1 hour or until brown. Yield: 12 servings.

Gail Dixon
Lyons Jr. H.S., Vidalia, GA

Dan's Shrimp

1½ c. packed brown sugar
⅓ c. cornstarch
2 tsp. salt
⅔ c. vinegar
½ c. (or more) water
2 green peppers, thinly sliced
1½ c. drained pineapple tidbits
2   20-oz. packages frozen breaded
     fantail shrimp
Oil for deep frying

Mix brown sug...
saucepan. Sti...
low heat unti...
Cook, covere...
pepper and ...
through. De...
directions; ...
sauce over ...
Yield: 12 servings.

Goshen H.S., Goshen,...

56 / Seafood

Seafood-Wil...
1   6-oz.
     and
1 lb.
1 ...
1 ...

Shrimp Casserole

4 c. cooked rice
2   4-oz. jars chopped pimento
2 sm. onions, grated
2   7-oz. cans sliced water chestnuts,
     drained
2 c. mayonnaise
2 cans cream of mushroom soup
2 cans tomato soup
2   4-oz. cans sliced mushrooms, drained
Salt and pepper to taste
2½ lb. shrimp, cleaned, cooked
3 c. shredded sharp cheese
Paprika

Combine rice, pimento, onions and water chestnuts in bowl; mix well. Spoon into buttered 4-quart baking dish. Combine mayonnaise, soups, mushrooms, salt and pepper in bowl. Layer half the soup mixture, shrimp and remaining soup mixture over rice mixture. Top with cheese. Sprinkle with paprika. Bake at 350 degrees for 35 minutes. Yield: 16 servings.

Millie Morris
Richmond Hill H.S., Richmond Hill, GA

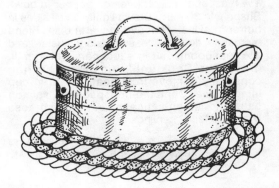

Rice Casserole

package long grain
wild rice mix
crab meat, drained
... peeled shrimp, drained
⅓ c. grated onion
1 c. chopped green pepper
1 c. chopped celery
1 4-oz. jar pimento, drained
2 tbsp. lemon juice
3 cans cream of mushroom soup

Prepare rice according to package directions; drain. Combine with remaining ingredients in bowl; mix well. Spoon into lightly greased 4-quart baking dish. Bake at 325 degrees for 1 hour. Yield: 12 servings.

Harriett McCallister
Kempsville Jr. H.S., Virginia Beach, VA

Spaghetti with Salmon Balls

2 15-oz. cans salmon, drained, flaked
4 c. soft bread crumbs
4 eggs, slightly beaten
3 tbsp. lemon juice
2 tsp. dry mustard
1½ tsp. salt
1 tbsp. lemon pepper
¼ c. butter
½ c. melted margarine
½ c. flour
1½ tsp. each dry mustard, salt
5 c. milk
¼ c. lemon juice
32 oz. thin spaghetti, cooked

Mix salmon with bread crumbs, eggs, 3 table-spoons lemon juice, 2 teaspoons dry mustard, 1½ teaspoons salt and lemon pepper in bowl. Shape into 30 balls. Brown lightly on all sides in butter in skillet. Remove to warm dish. Blend margarine, flour, 1½ teaspoons dry mustard and 1½ teaspoons salt in saucepan. Stir in milk gradually. Cook until thickened, stirring constantly; remove from heat. Stir in ¼ cup lemon juice. Combine hot spaghetti, salmon balls and lemon sauce in serving dish; toss lightly. Yield: 12 servings.

Donna Dyess
Crystal Springs H.S., Crystal Springs, MS

Tuna Chow Mein

8 c. chopped celery
4 c. chopped onions
2 c. chopped green pepper
½ c. margarine
5 cans mushroom soup
2 c. milk
12 7-oz. cans tuna, drained
1 c. chopped pimento
2 tbsp. soy sauce
1 tsp. MSG
Pepper to taste
4 3-oz. cans chow mein noodles

Sauté celery, onions and green pepper in margarine in large saucepan for 5 minutes. Stir in soup and milk. Add tuna, pimento, soy sauce, MSG and pepper. Cook until heated through, mixing gently. Spoon into shallow baking dishes. Bake at 350 degrees for 30 minutes. Serve with chow mein noodles. Yield: 24 servings.

Barbara J. Bird
Alma H.S., Alma, MI

Tuna-Noodle Bake

4 cans cream of mushroom soup
2 c. water
2 c. grated Cheddar cheese
1 tsp. Worcestershire sauce
4 cans tuna, drained, flaked
1 16-oz. package medium noodles, cooked
1 c. fine cracker crumbs
¼ c. butter
6 hard-boiled eggs, sliced

Heat soup and water in saucepan over medium heat. Add cheese and Worcestershire sauce. Stir until smooth; remove from heat. Add tuna and noodles; mix well. Pour into greased 3-quart casserole. Sprinkle with cracker crumbs; dot with butter. Bake at 350 degrees for 40 minutes. Top with eggs. Bake 5 to 10 minutes longer. Yield: 16 servings.

Anna Brandon
Fort Worth, TX

Breakfast Cheese Puff

10 slices day-old bread, cubed
8 oz. ham, chopped
8 eggs
2½ c. milk
1 can cream of mushroom soup
1 tsp. dry mustard
1 tsp. salt
¼ tsp. pepper
2 tbsp. butter
1½ c. grated sharp Cheddar cheese

Layer bread cubes and ham in greased 9x13-inch baking dish. Combine eggs, milk, soup and seasonings in mixer bowl or blender; beat or process until smooth. Pour over bread and ham. Dot with butter. Sprinkle with cheese. Chill for several hours to overnight. Bake at 350 degrees for 40 to 45 minutes or until set. Serve immediately. Yield: 16 servings.

Esther P. Gelatt
Honesdale H.S., Honesdale, PA

Breakfast Soufflé

1 lb. hot sausage
1 lb. regular sausage
12 eggs
4 c. milk
2 tsp. salt
2 tsp. dry mustard
4 slices bread
2 c. shredded Cheddar cheese

Brown sausage in skillet, stirring until crumbly; drain on paper towels. Combine eggs, milk, salt and dry mustard in bowl; mix well but do not beat. Crumble bread into egg mixture. Add sausage and cheese; mix gently. Pour into greased 9x13-inch baking dish. Chill overnight. Bake at 350 degrees for 30 to 45 minutes or until set. Let stand for 10 minutes before serving. Yield: 12 servings.

Trudy K. Miller
Bishop Carroll H.S., Wichita, KS

Buffet Eggs Deluxe

4 lb. pork sausage
24 slices bread, cubed
6 c. shredded Cheddar cheese
18 eggs, beaten
7½ c. milk
2¼ tsp. dry mustard
3 cans mushroom soup
1½ c. milk

Brown sausage in skillet, stirring until crumbly; drain. Layer bread, cheese and sausage in 2 greased 9x13-inch baking dishes. Combine eggs, 7½ cups milk and dry mustard in bowl; mix well. Pour over layers. Chill, covered, overnight. Mix soup and 1½ cups milk in bowls. Pour over casseroles. Bake at 300 degrees for 1½ hours. Let stand for 5 minutes before cutting into squares. Yield: 24 servings.

Pamela Meyer
Augusta H.S., Augusta, WI

Brunch Casserole

1 stick margarine
8 oz. Cheddar cheese, sliced
1 green pepper, cut into strips
1 c. sliced fresh mushrooms
3 or 4 tomatoes, sliced
1 lb. bacon, crisp-fried, crumbled
12 eggs
¼ c. water
1 tsp. dry mustard
Salt and pepper to taste

Slice margarine into 9x13-inch baking dish. Layer cheese, green pepper, mushrooms, tomatoes and bacon in prepared dish. Combine eggs and remaining ingredients in bowl; beat with wire whisk. Pour over layers. Bake at 325 degrees for 45 to 60 minutes or until set. Yield: 12 servings.

Linda Finley
Harrison Central Ninth Gr. Sch., Gulfport, MS

Mrs. B's Fluffy Eggs

12 slices bread
Butter, softened
6 eggs
3 c. milk
½ tsp. dry mustard
1 tsp. salt
1½ c. shredded Swiss cheese
1½ c. shredded Cheddar cheese

Trim crusts from bread. Spread 1 side with butter; cut into cubes. Sprinkle in 9x12-inch baking dish. Combine eggs, milk, dry mustard and salt in bowl; mix well. Pour over bread. Sprinkle cheeses over top. Chill, covered, overnight. Bake at 325 degrees for 1 hour. Yield: 12 servings.

Annmarie Milnamow
St. Edward H.S., Elgin, IL

Cheese Enchiladas

½ c. margarine, melted
¼ c. flour
¼ c. chili mix
2 8-oz. cans tomato sauce
4 c. water
2 7-oz. packages corn tortillas
24 process cheese slices

Combine margarine, flour, chili mix, tomato sauce and water in saucepan; mix well. Bring to a boil. Dip each tortilla in sauce to soften. Roll 1 slice cheese in each tortilla. Arrange in 2 lightly greased 9-inch baking dishes. Pour remaining sauce over tortillas. Bake at 350 degrees for 20 minutes. Yield: 12 servings.

Millie Sawyn
Irving, TX

Green Chili Quiche

10 eggs
1 16-oz. carton cottage cheese
1 tsp. baking powder
1 tsp. salt
10 drops of Tabasco sauce
½ c. flour
1 tbsp. onion flakes
Dash of garlic powder
1 lb. Monterey Jack cheese, shredded
1 7-oz. can chopped green chilies
½ c. butter, melted

Process first 8 ingredients in blender container until smooth. Mix with cheese, chilies and butter in bowl. Pour into buttered 9x13-inch baking dish. Bake at 400 degrees for 15 minutes. Reduce temperature to 350 degrees. Bake for 25 to 30 minutes or until set. Cut into squares. Yield: 12 servings.

Betty Pitts
Sierra Vista Jr. H.S., Canyon Country, CA

Egg-Sausage Strata

3 lb. sliced bread
4 lb. sausage
2½ lb. Cheddar cheese, grated
42 eggs
3 qt. milk
1½ tbsp. dry mustard
1 tbsp. salt
1 tsp. pepper

Trim crusts from bread; cut into cubes. Brown sausage in skillet, stirring until crumbly; drain. Layer bread cubes, sausage and cheese in 2 greased 12x20-inch baking pans. Combine remaining ingredients in large bowl; beat until smooth. Pour over layers. Chill, covered, for 12 hours to overnight. Bake for 1 hour or until set. Cut into squares. Garnish squares with cherry tomato or tomato slice. Yield: 36 servings.

Sharon Coward
Ocean Springs H.S., Ocean Springs, MS

Sausage Casserole

2 lb. sausage
16 slices bread, crusts trimmed
3 c. shredded Cheddar cheese
8 eggs
5½ c. milk
2 cans mushroom soup
1 tsp. prepared mustard
2 tsp. salt
1 tsp. pepper

Brown sausage in skillet, stirring until crumbly; drain. Layer bread slices, sausage and cheese in two 9x13-inch baking dishes. Combine eggs and remaining ingredients in bowl; mix well. Pour over layers. Chill for 8 hours to overnight. Bake at 325 degrees for 1 hour. Yield: 12-14 servings.

Kathy Thomas
Chickasha Mid. Sch., Chickasha, OK

VEGETABLES
AND
SIDE DISHES

Asparagus Casserole

2 cans cut asparagus, drained
1 can early peas, drained
1 3 to 4-oz. can water chestnuts
1 3-oz. can mushrooms, chopped
10 oz. cheese, shredded
2 cans mushroom soup
5 slices bread, toasted, crumbled
Melted butter

Drain asparagus, reserving ¾ cup liquid. Drain peas, reserving ¼ cup liquid. Layer vegetables, cheese and soup ½ at a time in buttered 9x13-inch baking dish. Pour reserved liquid over top. Mix toasted crumbs with enough butter to moisten. Sprinkle over layers. Bake at 300 degrees for 40 minutes or until bubbly. Yield: 16 servings.

Anita Jenkins
Akron, OH

Baked Beans

16 c. dried beans
1 lb. ham, chopped
4 onions, chopped
2 c. molasses
2 c. packed brown sugar
1½ tsp. dry mustard
¼ c. salt

Soak beans in water to cover in large electric roaster overnight. Cook in same water at 300 degrees until tender. Add ham and onions. Combine remaining ingredients in small bowl. Stir into beans. Cook at 250 degrees for 5 hours or to desired consistency. Yield: 100 servings.

Bobbie D. Smith
Waynoka H.S., Waynoka, OK

Closed-Pit Baked Beans

8 lb. navy beans
2 c. sugar
4 lb. salt pork, cubed
8 c. tomato juice
1 c. molasses
16 c. water

Mix all ingredients in 5 to 8-gallon stainless steel pail with cover. Place in corner of barbecue pit. Bank with 18 inches hot coals. Cook until beans are tender. May add catsup if necessary to make of desired consistency. Yield: 100 servings.

Harlan Hogue
Jackson's Mill, WV

Easy Baked Beans

4 32-oz. cans pork and beans
1 c. packed brown sugar
2 c. catsup
½ to ¾ c. chopped onion
16 slices bacon, chopped
3 tbsp. Worcestershire sauce
2 tsp. dry mustard

Combine all ingredients in large bowl; mix well. Place in large shallow roasting pan. Bake, covered with foil, at 350 degrees for 45 minutes. Bake, uncovered, for 1¼ hours or to desired consistency, adding a small amount of water if necessary. Yield: 15 servings.

Diane Zook
Larned H.S., Larned, KS

Chuck Wagon Beans

2 lb. dried pinto beans
12 c. water
2 bunches green onions, chopped
1½ lb. ham, chopped
4 dashes of Worcestershire sauce
¼ tsp. garlic salt
1½ tsp. each seasoned salt, pepper

Combine beans and water in large saucepan. Add remaining ingredients. Cook over medium heat for 2 hours. Simmer for 1 hour longer or until beans are tender. Yield: 16 servings.

Maude Simmons
El Paso, TX

Savory Baked Beans

1 c. packed dark brown sugar
½ c. molasses
½ c. vinegar
¼ c. barbecue sauce
4 med. onions, chopped
2 tsp. dry mustard
1½ tsp. chili powder
1 tsp. garlic powder
2 tsp. salt
1   16-oz. can pork and beans
1   16-oz. can kidney beans, drained
1   16-oz. can lima beans, drained
1   16-oz. can wax beans, drained
8 slices crisp-fried bacon, crumbled

Combine first 9 ingredients in large saucepan; mix well. Simmer for 20 minutes. Add beans and bacon; mix well. Spoon into 9x13-inch baking dish. Bake at 350 degrees for 1 hour. Yield: 12 servings.
Note: May cook in slow cooker on Low for 4 hours or to desired consistency.

Ann McMullin
Smith Cotton H.S., Sedalia, MO

Suicide Beans

1 gal. pinto beans
1 gal. ranch-style beans
2 onions, chopped
10 jalapeño peppers, chopped
2 lg. green peppers, chopped
3 cloves of garlic, chopped
1 can Ro-Tel tomatoes, chopped
1½ oz. chili powder
½ bottle of Worcestershire sauce
3 tbsp. red hot sauce

Combine beans, onions, jalapeño peppers, green peppers, garlic, Ro-Tel tomatoes and seasonings in bean pot; mix well. Cook over medium heat until onions are tender.
Yield: 70 servings.

Paul Matthews
Alexandria, LA

Cheddar Carrots

3 lb. carrots, peeled, sliced
3 lg. onions, sliced
3 tbsp. margarine
1 lb. longhorn cheese, shredded
1 lb. Cheddar cheese, shredded
1 c. seasoned bread crumbs

Cook carrots in water to cover in saucepan until tender; drain. Sauté onions in margarine in skillet until tender. Stir in carrots. Mix cheeses together. Layer half the carrot mixture, half the cheese mixture and remaining carrot mixture in 3-quart baking dish. Add crumbs to remaining cheese mixture; mix well. Sprinkle over casserole. Bake at 350 degrees for 45 minutes to 1 hour or until light brown. Yield: 12 servings.

Charnelle Ebert
Mineral, WV

Scalloped Carrots

10 carrots, peeled, sliced
1 med. onion, minced
2 tbsp. butter
3 tbsp. flour
½ tsp. salt
¼ tsp. dry mustard
⅛ tsp. each pepper, celery salt
1 c. milk
6 oz. Cheddar cheese, sliced
3 tbsp. bread crumbs

Cook carrots in a small amount of water in saucepan until tender-crisp; drain, reserving liquid. Sauté onion in butter in skillet for 2 to 3 minutes. Blend in flour and seasonings. Stir in milk gradually. Cook until smooth and thickened, stirring constantly and adding ¼ cup reserved carrot liquid if necessary. Alternate layers of carrots and cheese in casserole until all ingredients are used. Pour sauce over layers. Sprinkle with crumbs. Bake at 350 degrees for 25 minutes. Yield: 12-15 servings.

Tina Kimble
Hydro, OK

Broccoli-Corn Jubilee

4   16-oz. cans cream-style corn
2   10-oz. packages frozen chopped
    broccoli, thawed
2 eggs, beaten
1⅓ c. cracker crumbs
2 tbsp. minced onion
2 tbsp. melted butter

Combine all ingredients in bowl; mix well. Spoon into greased casserole. Bake at 350 degrees for 35 to 40 minutes. Yield: 12-14 servings.

Becky Schilling
Brown, MI

Corn Casserole

1 lb. bacon
1½ c. chopped onion
1 lg. green pepper, chopped
1 c. chopped celery
3   16-oz. cans cream-style corn
3   12-oz. cans whole kernel corn, drained
Salt and pepper to taste
1 c. cracker crumbs
Chopped pimento

Fry bacon in skillet until crisp; drain reserving a small amount of drippings. Sauté onion, green pepper and celery in reserved drippings. Add corn, crumbled bacon, seasonings and half the cracker crumbs; mix well. Spoon into buttered 3-quart baking dish. Top with remaining crumbs and pimento. Bake at 350 degrees until bubbly. Yield: 18-20 servings.

Ella Jo Adams
Allen H.S., Allen, TX

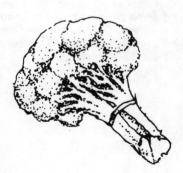

Corn Pudding

3 cans yellow cream-style corn
2 eggs, beaten
¾ c. yellow cornmeal
½ tsp. garlic salt
½ c. oil
½ tsp. baking powder
1   4-oz. can chopped green chilies
2 c. shredded Cheddar cheese

Combine first 7 ingredients with ⅔ of the cheese in bowl; mix well. Pour into greased baking dish. Top with remaining cheese. Bake at 350 degrees for 45 minutes. Yield: 12-15 servings.

Candy Gray
Stillwater, OK

Different and Delicious Corn

2 sticks margarine
16-oz. cream cheese, softened
2   16-oz. cans whole kernel corn
2   16-oz. cans Shoe Peg corn
2   12-oz. cans Mexicorn
2   16-oz. cans cream-style corn

Melt margarine and cream cheese in large saucepan over low heat, stirring until smooth. Drain whole kernel, Shoe Peg and Mexicorn, reserving a small amount of liquid. Add drained and cream-style corn to cream cheese mixture; mix well. Stir in enough reserved liquid to make of desired consistency. Cook over low heat until heated through, stirring frequently. Yield: 16 servings.

Cecelia Bowers
Ashville, NC

Fresh Corn Bake

18 c. freshly cut corn
2 c. half and half
1 lb. butter, melted

Combine all ingredients in large baking pan; mix well. Bake at 325 degrees for 1 hour, stirring occasionally. Yield: 25 servings.

Arlene Moen
Pope, MN

Make and Store Cucumbers

12 med. cucumbers, thinly sliced
1 green pepper, chopped
1 red pepper, chopped
8 sm. onions, sliced
½ c. chopped celery
¼ c. canning salt
2 c. white vinegar
2½ c. sugar

Combine vegetables and salt in large bowl; mix well. Let stand for 2 hours. Drain in colander. Rinse under running water; drain. Combine vinegar and sugar in saucepan. Bring to a boil; cool. Pour over cucumber mixture in large container. Store, covered, in refrigerator. Yield: 36 servings.

Joan Petersen
Mille Lacs, MN

Baked Onion Casserole

12 med. onions, thinly sliced
1   3¾ oz. bag potato chips, crushed
8 oz. mild cheese, shredded
2 cans cream of mushroom soup
½ c. milk
⅛ tsp. cayenne pepper

Layer onions, potato chips and cheese alternately in buttered 9x13-inch baking dish. Pour mixture of soup and milk over layers. Sprinkle with cayenne pepper. Bake at 350 degrees for 1 hour. Yield: 12 servings.

Erica Linsley
Kansas City, MO

Glorified Peas

3   10-oz. packages frozen peas, cooked, drained
1   4-oz. jar pimentos, chopped
1 c. milk
½ tsp. salt
2 tbsp. onion
1   8-oz. package cream cheese, softened

Combine peas and pimentos in buttered 9x13-inch baking pan; mix lightly. Combine milk, salt, onion and cream cheese in blender container.

Process until smooth. Pour over vegetables. Bake at 350 degrees for 30 minutes. Yield: 12 servings.

Jill Taylor
Urbana, IN

Cream Potatoes

2 lb. frozen Southern-style hashed brown potatoes
1 sm. onion, chopped
1   16-oz. carton sour cream
2 cans cream of potato soup
1 can cream of celery soup
2 c. shredded mozzarella cheese

Combine potatoes, onion, sour cream, soups and 1 cup cheese in bowl; mix well. Spoon into 9x13-inch baking dish. Top with remaining 1 cup cheese. Bake at 250 degrees for 2½ hours. Yield: 12 servings.

Mary Alice Lee
Kaukauna H.S., Hilbert, WI

Potatoes Supreme

2 lb. frozen hashed brown potatoes
½ c. chopped onion
1 can cream of chicken soup
½ c. melted margarine
1   16-oz. carton sour cream
2 c. shredded Cheddar cheese
1 tsp. salt
2 c. crushed cornflakes
¼ c. melted margarine

Combine potatoes, onion, soup, ½ cup margarine, sour cream, cheese and salt in bowl; mix well. Spoon into 9x13-inch baking dish. Mix cornflake crumbs with remaining ¼ cup margarine. Sprinkle over potatoes. Bake at 350 degrees for 1 hour. Yield: 12 servings.
Note: May prepare in advance and refrigerate for up to 24 hours before baking.

Mary Ann Hanson
Doniphan H.S., Doniphan, NE

Hashed Brown Casserole

2 lb. frozen hashed brown potatoes
½ c. chopped onion
2 c. sour cream
1 can mushroom soup
1 c. grated Cheddar cheese
½ c. melted butter
½ tsp. each salt and pepper
½ c. bread crumbs

Spread potatoes in 2-quart baking dish. Combine onion, sour cream, soup, cheese, butter and seasonings in bowl; mix well. Pour over potatoes. Sprinkle with bread crumbs. Bake at 350 degrees for 1 hour. Yield: 12 servings.

Delinda McCormick
Caldwell Co. H.S., Cadiz, KY

Hashed Brown Potato Casserole

2 lb. frozen hashed brown potatoes
½ c. chopped onion
1 can cream of chicken soup
10 oz. Cheddar cheese, grated
1 c. sour cream
¼ c. melted margarine
1 tsp. salt
½ tsp. pepper
1 to 2 c. butter cracker crumbs
¼ c. melted margarine

Combine first 8 ingredients in bowl; mix well. Spoon into greased 9x13-inch baking dish. Mix cracker crumbs with ¼ cup melted margarine in bowl. Sprinkle over potatoes. Bake at 350 degrees for 1 hour and 10 minutes. Yield: 12-14 servings.

Rebecca W. Harrell
Franklin-Simpson Mid. Sch., Franklin, KY

Potato Pancakes

2 lb. Idaho potatoes, peeled
2 eggs, beaten
¼ c. grated onion
2 tbsp. flour
¾ tsp. salt
Dash each of nutmeg, pepper
Oil for frying

Grate potatoes coarsely into large bowl filled with ice water. Let stand for 15 minutes. Beat eggs with onion, flour and seasonings in large bowl. Drain potatoes; pat dry. Stir 4 cups potatoes into egg mixture. Pour by ¼ cupfuls into ⅛-inch deep very hot oil in heavy skillet. Do not crowd. Fry for 2 to 3 minutes on each side or until brown and crisp; drain on paper towels. Yield: 12 servings.

Mildred Robinson
Marshall, WV

Cheesy Scalloped Potatoes

1 onion, chopped
4 oz. bacon, crisp-fried, crumbled
12 c. thinly sliced peeled potatoes
10-oz. extra-sharp cheese, sliced
2 tbsp. margarine

Combine onion and bacon in small bowl. Alternate layers of potatoes, onion mixture and cheese in foil-lined 9x13-inch baking dish, ending with potatoes. Dot with margarine. Bake, tightly covered, at 400 degrees for 1½ hours or until potatoes are tender. Yield: 25 servings.

Mildred S. Bleiler
Lehigh, PA

Party Scalloped Potatoes

20 lb. potatoes, cooked, chilled
1 c. melted butter
1 c. flour
3 tbsp. salt
Pepper to taste
¼ c. instant onions
1 gal. milk
¼ c. minced parsley

Peel and slice potatoes; place in large baking pan. Blend butter and flour in saucepan. Mix in salt, pepper and onions. Stir in milk gradually. Cook until thickened, stirring constantly. Stir in parsley. Pour over potatoes. Bake at 325 degrees for 1 hour or until heated through. Yield: 25 servings.

Nell Odom
Newport News, VA

Polish Sauerkraut

1   20-oz. can sauerkraut
1 sm. head cabbage, shredded
6 lg. onions, sliced
2 qt. water
4 c. chicken broth
6 bay leaves
2 tbsp. sugar
3 tbsp. salt

Rinse and drain sauerkraut. Combine with remaining ingredients in large saucepan. Simmer for 1½ hours or to desired consistency. Remove bay leaves. Yield: 25 servings.

Marilyn Mancewicz
Ottawa Hills H.S., Grand Rapids, MI

Spinach Casserole

3   10-oz. packages frozen spinach
8 oz. cream cheese, chopped
2 tbsp. melted butter
1 sm. onion, minced
½ tsp. seasoned salt
⅛ tsp. pepper
1   8-oz. package seasoned stuffing mix
½ c. melted butter

Cook spinach according to package directions; drain well. Combine with cream cheese, 2 tablespoons butter, onion, salt and pepper in saucepan. Heat until cream cheese melts; mix well. Spoon into 9x13-inch baking dish. Sauté stuffing lightly in ½ cup margarine in skillet. Sprinkle over spinach. Bake at 350 degrees for 20 minutes. Yield: 12 servings.

Leslie K. Donnell
Talawanda H.S., Oxford, OH

Spinach Roll

2   10-oz. packages chopped spinach,
*   cooked, drained*
6 tbsp. melted butter
Dash of nutmeg
3 eggs, separated
1 c. chopped onion
15 fresh mushrooms, sliced
3 tbsp. butter
½ tsp. salt
Basil, parsley, pepper to taste
1½ c. grated Cheddar cheese

Combine spinach, 6 tablespooons butter, nutmeg and beaten egg yolks in bowl; mix well. Fold in stiffly beaten egg whites gently. Spread over greased baking sheet. Bake at 350 degrees for 20 minutes. Loosen edges with spatula. Invert onto foil. Sauté onion and mushrooms in 3 tablespoons butter in skillet. Stir in seasonings. Spread over spinach. Sprinkle with 1 cup cheese. Roll as for jelly roll. Place on baking sheet. Top with ½ cup cheese. Bake for 15 minutes longer. Yield: 12 servings.

Kim Terry
Amarillo, TX

Zucchini Casserole

18 med. zucchini, sliced, cooked
1½ c. shredded Cheddar cheese
3   4-oz. cans green chilies
Salt to taste
Bread crumbs
Margarine

Layer zucchini, cheese and green chilies in 2 baking dishes. Sprinkle with salt and bread crumbs. Dot with margarine. Bake at 350 degrees for 10 minutes or until bubbly. Yield: 18 servings.

Louise Blanco
Albuquerque, NM

M.J.'s Vegetable Casserole

2   10-oz. packages frozen mixed
*   vegetables*
2 c. each chopped celery, onion
2 c. sliced water chestnuts
2 c. mayonnaise
2 c. grated cheese
2 stacks butter crackers, crushed
2 sticks margarine, melted

Cook frozen vegetables according to package directions; drain. Combine celery, onion and water chestnuts in bowl. Add mixture of mayonnaise and cheese; mix well. Add mixed vegetables; mix lightly. Spoon into buttered 9x13-inch baking dish. Top with cracker crumbs and margarine. Bake at 375 degrees for 30 minutes or until bubbly. Yield: 12-16 servings.

Linda Finley
Harrison Central Ninth Gr. Sch., Gulfport, MS

Macaroni Fiesta

½ c. minced green pepper
2 tbsp. butter
2 tbsp. flour
2 c. milk
1 tsp. salt
¼ tsp. pepper
½ tsp. dry mustard
1 c. shredded cheese
½ c. sliced stuffed olives
1¾ c. macaroni, cooked
2 c. cornflakes
1 tbsp. melted butter
1 c. shredded cheese

Sauté green pepper in 2 tablespoons butter in saucepan until tender. Stir in flour. Stir in milk gradually. Cook until thickened, stirring constantly. Stir in seasonings and 1 cup cheese. Fold in olives and macaroni. Pour into 1½-quart baking dish. Toss cornflakes with 1 tablespoon melted butter. Sprinkle over casserole. Top with remaining 1 cup cheese. Bake at 350 degrees for 20 minutes or until heated through. Yield: 12 servings.

Cynthia Haviland
Stephens, OK

Cheese Grits Casserole

2 c. uncooked grits
8 c. boiling salted water
1 roll smoky cheese or jalapeño cheese
2 tbsp. Worcestershire sauce
2 eggs, beaten
2 tbsp. cooking Sherry
Dash of Tabasco sauce
2 sticks butter, melted
Pinch of paprika

Cook grits in boiling salted water according to package directions. Add cheese, Worcestershire sauce, eggs, Sherry and Tabasco sauce; mix well. Spoon into 2 baking dishes. Drizzle with butter. Sprinkle with paprika. Bake at 325 degrees for 1 hour. Yield: 12 servings.

Frances Berry
Arlington, VA

Baked Cheese Grits

5 c. milk
1½ c. uncooked grits
1 c. butter
⅔ c. Parmesan cheese
2 5-oz. jars sharp process cheese spread
1 tsp. salt

Bring milk to a boil in saucepan. Stir in grits. Cook for 10 minutes or until thickened, stirring frequently. Add remaining ingredients; mix well. Spoon into greased 2-quart baking dish. Bake at 350 degrees for 20 minutes. Yield: 12 servings.

Kathy Thomas
Chickasha Mid. Sch., Chickasha, OK

Golden Cheese Grits

1½ c. uncooked grits
6 c. water
3 eggs, beaten
1½ sticks butter
1 lb. Cheddar cheese, grated
2 tsp. salt
1 tsp. Tabasco sauce

Cook grits in boiling water in saucepan. Stir in remaining ingredients. Pour into 9x13-inch baking dish. Bake at 250 degrees for 1 hour. Garnish with paprika. Yield: 15 servings.

Anne Hargrow
Gadsden, AL

Jalapeño Rice

½ c. chopped celery
1 onion, chopped
1 green pepper, chopped
½ c. margarine
4 c. water
4 beef bouillon cubes
6 tbsp. chopped jalapeño peppers
2 c. uncooked rice
1 c. shredded cheese

Sauté vegetables in margarine in skillet. Add water, bouillon cubes and jalapeño peppers. Bring to a boil. Pour over rice in two 9x13-inch baking dishes. Top with cheese. Bake, covered, at 350 degrees for 1 hour. Yield: 12 servings.

Joann Hedrick
Luling, TX

Creamy Lemon Rice

2 sticks butter
4 c. long grain rice
Grated rind of 4 lemons
6 c. chicken stock
2 tsp. salt
¼ c. lemon juice
2 c. heavy cream
Freshly ground pepper to taste

Melt butter in heavy saucepan. Add rice and lemon rind. Sauté over medium heat for 5 minutes or until rice is opaque. Bring chicken stock to a boil in saucepan. Add stock and salt to rice. Simmer, covered, for 20 minutes or until broth is absorbed. Stir in lemon juice and cream gradually. Simmer for 5 minutes or until cream is absorbed, stirring constantly. Season with pepper. Yield: 12 servings.

Jane Bigler
Hillcrest Jr. H.S., Lenexa, KS

Green Rice

2 c. rice
8 oz. sharp cheese, grated
1⅓ c. chopped parsley
3 eggs, slightly beaten
2⅓ c. evaporated milk
2 cloves of garlic, chopped
⅓ tsp. MSG
1 tsp. seasoned salt
⅔ tsp. pepper
1⅓ tsp. salt
1 tbsp. lemon juice
1 tsp. grated lemon rind
1⅓ c. oil
Paprika to taste

Cook rice according to package directions. Combine with cheese and parsley in bowl; mix well. Combine eggs, evaporated milk, garlic, MSG, seasoned salt, pepper, salt, lemon juice and rind in mixer bowl; mix well. Add oil gradually, beating until smooth. Fold into rice mixture. Pour into two 2½-quart casseroles. Sprinkle with paprika. Place in shallow pan of water. Bake at 350 degrees for 1 hour. Yield: 16 servings.

Maxie DeLaney
Paris, MO

Springtime Rice

2 c. rice
¼ c. olive oil
1 c. chopped green pepper
1 c. chopped spring onions
1 to 2 c. sliced mushrooms
¼ c. parsley flakes
4 to 5 c. chicken broth

Sauté rice in oil in large skillet over medium heat until lightly browned. Add green pepper, onions and mushrooms. Sauté for 1 to 2 minutes. Pour into 2-quart casserole. Add chicken broth. Bake, covered, at 350 degrees for 35 to 45 minutes or until liquid is absorbed. Toss well. Yield: 12 servings.

Susan Milholland
Wilkesboro, NC

Grandmother Fold's Dressing

1 sm. bunch celery, chopped
5 med. onions, chopped
½ c. margarine
¾ c. cooked oatmeal
1 sm. box cornflakes
10 slices bread, crumbled
1½ stacks crackers, crushed
½ c. margarine
1 chicken bouillon cube
2 qt. (about) chicken stock
12 eggs, well beaten

Sauté celery and onions in ½ cup margarine in skillet. Combine with oatmeal, cornflakes, bread crumbs and cracker crumbs in large bowl; mix well. Add ½ cup melted margarine and bouillon dissolved in chicken stock; mix well. Beat in eggs. Mixture should resemble cake batter. Pour into 3 greased 9x13-inch baking dishes. Bake at 350 degrees until set and brown. Yield: 24-30 servings.

Danna Sue Hadsock
Appling Co. Jr. H.S., Baxley, GA

Bread Stuffing

2½ c. minced onion
3 c. chopped celery
3 c. butter
18 c. soft bread cubes
4 tsp. salt
1 tbsp. sage
2 tsp. thyme
1½ tsp. pepper

Sauté onion and celery in butter in large skillet. Stir in bread cubes and seasonings. Shape into balls. Place on baking sheets. Bake at 350 degrees for 45 minutes. Yield: 20 servings.

Nancy Womack
Daleville, VA

Pineapple-Cheese Casserole

2 lg. cans pineapple chunks
2 c. shredded Cheddar cheese
1 c. sugar
6 tbsp. flour
20 to 25 Ritz crackers, crushed
1 stick margarine, melted

Drain 1 can pineapple. Combine drained pineapple, undrained pineapple and cheese in bowl; mix well. Add mixture of sugar and flour. Pour into baking dish. Sprinkle crackers over top. Drizzle with margarine. Bake at 350 degrees for 30 minutes. Yield: 12 servings.

Virginia Gray
Lexington, KY

Hot Fruit Casserole

¾ c. packed brown sugar
6 tbsp. margarine
1 lg. can peach halves, drained
1 lg. can pear halves, drained
1 can pineapple chunks, drained
1 can apricots, drained
1 sm. jar maraschino cherries, drained

Sprinkle brown sugar in 9x13-inch baking dish; dot with margarine. Arrange fruit in prepared dish. Bake, covered, at 350 degrees for 1 hour. Serve warm. Yield: 12 servings.

Agnes Bowman
Columbia, SC

Hot Gingered Fruit

1 28-oz. can cling peach halves
1 28-oz. can whole pitted apricots
1 28-oz. can pineapple slices
1 28-oz. can pear halves
¼ c. butter, melted
½ tsp. ginger
¾ c. packed brown sugar
2 tbsp. pineapple juice

Drain fruit; pat dry with paper towels. Arrange in greased 2-quart casserole. Blend remaining ingredients in small saucepan. Heat until brown sugar dissolves. Pour over fruit. Bake at 325 degrees for 40 minutes. Yield: 12 servings.

Karen Mitchell
St. Joseph, MO

Hot Brandied Fruit

1 30-oz. can apricot halves
1 29-oz. can pear halves
1 29-oz. can peach halves
1 20-oz. can sliced pineapple
1 16-oz. can Queen Anne cherries
1 16-oz. can dark sweet cherries
½ c. melted margarine
¾ c. packed brown sugar
1 tsp. ginger
10 whole cloves
4 cinnamon sticks

Drain fruit. Combine fruit in 2½-quart baking dish. Blend margarine and brown sugar in saucepan. Stir in spices. Pour over fruit. Bake at 325 degrees for 30 minutes. Remove cinnamon sticks. Yield: 12 servings.

Kathy Thomas
Chickasha Mid. Sch., Chickasha, OK

BREADS

Angel Biscuits

6 c. buttermilk baking mix
¼ c. sugar
1 pkg. dry yeast
⅓ c. shortening
1¼ to 2 c. milk
Margarine, melted

Combine first 3 ingredients in bowl. Cut in shortening until crumbly. Stir in enough milk to make soft dough. Roll ½ inch thick on lightly floured surface. Cut with biscuit cutter. Place on greased baking sheet. Brush with margarine. Bake at 425 degrees for 10 to 12 minutes or until golden brown. Yield: 30-36 biscuits.

Joni Sturm
Muenster, TX

Devonshire Scones

4 c. self-rising flour
1 tsp. salt
1 stick butter, softened
¼ c. sugar
1 c. milk
1 egg, beaten

Sift flour and salt into bowl. Cut in butter until crumbly. Stir in sugar and milk. Roll ½ inch thick on lightly floured surface. Cut with 2½-inch cutter. Place on greased baking sheet. Brush with egg. Bake at 400 degrees for 8 minutes or until golden. Cool on wire rack. Serve with butter, cream and preserves. Yield: 20 scones.

Phyllis Rice Capen
Port Orange, FL

Whole Wheat Biscuits

2 c. all-purpose flour
1 c. whole wheat flour
¼ c. sugar
5 tsp. baking powder
1 tsp. salt
1 c. milk
6 tbsp. oil

Combine dry ingredients in bowl. Mix milk and oil in small bowl. Add to dry ingredients; mix just until moistened. Knead lightly 3 or 4 times on floured surface. Roll ½-inch thick; cut with biscuit cutter. Place on ungreased baking sheet. Bake at 400 degrees for 12 to 15 minutes. Yield: 16 biscuits.

Linda Finley
Harrison Central Ninth Gr. Sch., Gulfport, MS

Company Coffee Cake

1 c. oil
4 eggs, beaten
1½ c. milk
2 c. sour cream
6 c. sifted flour
3 c. sugar
8 tsp. baking powder
2 tsp. salt
¼ c. flour
1 c. packed brown sugar
4 tsp. cinnamon
¼ c. melted butter
2 c. chopped pecans

Mix oil, eggs, milk and sour cream in bowl. Sift in 6 cups flour, sugar, baking powder and salt; mix well. Pour into greased 12 x 22-inch baking pan. Mix remaining ingredients in bowl. Sprinkle over batter. Bake at 350 degrees for 30 minutes or until coffee cake tests done. Yield: 40 servings.

Shirley Bolner
Jackson's Mill, WV

Fruit Swirl Coffee Cake

1½ c. sugar
½ c. each margarine, shortening
1½ tsp. baking powder
1 tsp. each vanilla, almond extract
4 eggs
3 c. flour
1 can cherry pie filling
1 c. confectioners' sugar
1 to 2 tbsp. milk

Combine first 7 ingredients in mixer bowl. Beat at low speed until blended, scraping bowl. Beat at high speed for 3 minutes. Stir in flour. Spread ⅔ of the batter in greased 10x15-inch baking pan. Top with pie filling. Drop remaining batter by tablespoonfuls over filling. Bake at 350 degrees for 45 minutes. Drizzle with mixture of confectioners' sugar and milk. Yield: 30 servings.

Toni Sewell
Ft. Wayne, IN

Corn Bread

4 c. self-rising cornmeal
1½ c. cold milk
4 eggs
1 c. melted shortening

Combine cornmeal, milk and eggs in bowl; mix well. Stir in shortening. Pour into greased 9x13-inch baking pan. Bake at 425 degrees for 40 minutes. Yield: 15-20 servings.

Lois Webber
East Forsyth H.S., Kernersville, NC

Tasty Doughnuts

4 c. sifted flour
4 tsp. baking powder
½ tsp. salt
¼ tsp. nutmeg
1 c. sugar
2 eggs, well beaten
¼ tsp. lemon extract
2 tbsp. butter, softened
1 c. milk
Oil for deep frying

Sift first 4 ingredients together 3 times. Combine sugar, eggs, flavoring and butter in bowl; mix well. Add sifted dry ingredients alternately with milk, mixing well after each addition. Knead lightly on floured surface. Roll ⅓-inch thick. Cut with floured doughnut cutter. Deep-fry in 385-degree oil until golden brown, turning frequently. Drain on paper towels. Sprinkle with additional sugar. Yield: 48 doughnuts.

Sandra Marion
Yanceyville, NC

Pumpkin Bread Quartet

3½ c. flour
1 tsp. each cinnamon, nutmeg
2 tsp. baking powder
1 c. oil
2 c. pumpkin
3½ c. sugar
1 tsp. soda
1½ tsp. salt
4 eggs
⅔ c. water
Chopped nuts

Combine all ingredients except nuts in mixer bowl. Beat until smooth. Stir in nuts. Pour into 4 greased loaf pans. Bake at 350 degrees for 50 to 60 minutes or until loaves test done. Cool on wire rack. Yield: 4 loaves.

Sharon Fowler
Nashville, TN

Quick Whole Wheat Bread

4 c. whole wheat flour
2 tsp. baking powder
2 tsp. soda
2 tsp. salt
1 c. packed brown sugar
3 c. buttermilk
2 eggs, beaten
½ c. melted butter

Combine all ingredients in bowl; mix well. Spoon into 2 well-greased 5x9-inch loaf pans. Brush additional butter over top. Bake at 350 degrees for 50 minutes. Remove to wire rack to cool. Yield: 2 loaves.

Betty Mabry
Bryan, TX

Blueberry Muffins

2 eggs
2 c. sugar
2 c. sour cream
½ c. oil
3½ c. flour
2 tsp. soda
½ tsp. salt
2 c. blueberries

Blend eggs, sugar, sour cream and oil in bowl. Sift dry ingredients together. Add to egg mixture; stir just until moistened. Fold in blueberries. Spoon into greased muffin cups. Bake at 350 degrees for 25 minutes. Yield: 24 muffins.

Kathy Thomas
Chickasha Mid. Sch., Chickasha, OK

Buttermilk Bran Muffins

5 c. flour
3 c. sugar
¼ c. soda
1 tbsp. salt
1 c. oil
4 eggs
1 qt. buttermilk
1 15-oz. box raisin bran cereal

Mix first 4 ingredients in bowl. Stir in oil, eggs, buttermilk and raisin bran. Fill greased muffin cups ⅔ full. Bake at 400 degrees for 20 minutes. Yield: 96 muffins.
Note: Batter may be stored in refrigerator for up to 6 weeks.

Jamie Comer
Tacoma, WA

Microwave Bran Raisin Muffins

2 tbsp. lemon juice
2 c. milk
2½ c. flour
1½ c. sugar
2½ tsp. soda
1 tsp. cinnamon
1 tsp. salt
2 eggs, slightly beaten
½ c. oil
3½ c. raisin bran cereal

Stir lemon juice into milk; set aside. Combine dry ingredients in bowl. Add eggs, oil and milk mixture; mix just until moistened. Stir in cereal. Store, covered, in refrigerator for 24 hours to 6 weeks. Fill paper-lined glass muffin cups half full. Microwave 6 at a time on Medium-High for 3½ to 4½ minutes or until muffins test done. Yield: 60 muffins.
Note: May microwave 2 muffins for 2 to 2½ minutes or 4 muffins for 2½ to 3½ minutes.

Sandra Whaley
North Whitfield Mid. Sch., Dalton, GA

Pancakes For-A-Crowd

10 lb. flour
8 c. dry milk powder
3¾ c. dried eggs
12½ c. sugar
⅔ c. baking powder
5 tbsp. salt
1½ gal. water
4 c. oil
2 tbsp. vanilla extract

Combine dry ingredients in very large container. Add water, oil and vanilla; mix just until moistened. Bake by ⅓ cupfuls on hot griddle until brown on both sides.
Yield: 200 four-inch pancakes.
Note: May substitute 18 fresh eggs for dried eggs and decrease water by 4 cups.

Teresa McGuire
Fairfield Comm. H.S., Fairfield, IL

Quick Wheat Mix

7 c. all-purpose flour
3 c. whole wheat flour
1 c. instant nonfat dry milk powder
⅓ c. baking powder
¼ c. sugar
1 tbsp. salt
2 c. shortening

Mix dry ingredients in bowl. Cut in shortening until crumbly. Store in airtight container at room temperature for up to 6 weeks.
Quick Wheat Biscuits: For each 8 biscuits, combine 1½ cups Mix with ⅓ cup water in bowl; mix with fork. Knead lightly 4 or 5 times on floured surface. Roll ½ inch thick. Cut with 2-inch biscuit cutter. Place on baking sheet. Bake at 425 degrees for 10 to 12 minutes or until brown.
Quick Mix Pancakes: For each 8 pancakes, combine 2 cups Mix with 1 cup milk or water and 1 beaten egg; stir just until moistened. Bake by ¼ cupfuls on hot greased griddle until light brown on both sides.

Katherine Anderson
East Central H.S., Lucedale, MS

Camp Bread

3 cakes yeast
4 c. warm milk
½ c. sugar
1 c. shortening
4 tsp. salt
3 eggs
13 to 14 c. flour

Dissolve yeast in 1 cup milk. Combine with remaining 3 cups milk, sugar, shortening, salt and eggs in mixer bowl; mix well. Mix in flour. Knead on floured surface for 6 to 8 minutes. Place in greased bowl, turning to grease surface. Let rise, covered, until doubled in bulk. Punch dough down. Let rise until almost doubled in bulk. Shape into 4 loaves; place in greased loaf pans. Let rise, covered, for 1 hour. Brush with butter. Bake at 400 degrees for 35 minutes or until loaves test done. Yield: 4 loaves.

George Loudenslager
Jacksons's Mill, WV

Health Bread

1 c. oats
2 tsp. salt
2 tbsp. shortening
1 c. raisins
1 c. 100% bran cereal
2¾ c. boiling water
2 pkg. dry yeast
½ c. warm water
¾ c. molasses
1 c. whole wheat flour
6 to 7 c. all-purpose flour

Combine first 6 ingredients in large bowl; mix well. Cool to lukewarm. Dissolve yeast in ½ cup warm water. Add to oat mixture with molasses; mix well. Stir in whole wheat flour and 2 cups all-purpose flour. Add enough remaining all-purpose flour to make soft dough; mix well. Knead on lightly floured surface for 10 to 12 minutes or until smooth and elastic. Place in greased bowl, turning to grease surface. Let rise, covered, in warm place for 1 hour or until doubled in bulk. Punch dough down. Let rest for 10 minutes. Shape into 3 loaves. Place in greased 5 x 9-inch loaf pans. Let rise in warm place for 45 minutes or until doubled in bulk. Bake at 350 degrees for 45 to 55 minutes or until bread tests done. Cool on wire rack. Yield: 3 loaves.

Nancy Bassett
Hyannis, MA

German Stollen Bread

1 c. shortening
1 c. (heaping) sugar
1 tbsp. salt
4 c. boiling water
1 c. milk
2 pkg. dry yeast
½ tsp. sugar
1 c. lukewarm water
5 lb. bread flour
1 egg
1½ tsp. cinnamon
1 c. chopped nuts
1 c. each raisins, currants, chopped
*   dates and candied fruit*
Melted butter
Cinnamon-sugar

Combine shortening, 1 cup sugar, salt and 4 cups boiling water in large bowl; mix until shortening is melted. Stir in milk. Cool to lukewarm. Dissolve yeast and ½ teaspoon sugar in 1 cup lukewarm water. Add to milk mixture. Add enough flour gradually to make of batter consistency. Stir in egg, cinnamon, nuts and fruit. Add enough remaining flour to make stiff dough. Knead on floured surface until smooth and elastic. Place in greased bowl, turning to grease surface. Let rise, covered, for 1½ to 2 hours or until doubled in bulk. Punch dough down. Let rise for 1 hour. Shape into 7 loaves. Place in greased loaf pans. Let rise until doubled in bulk. Bake at 375 degrees for 30 minutes. Brush with melted butter. Sprinkle with cinnamon-sugar. Yield: 7 loaves.
Note: This bread freezes well and is excellent sliced and toasted.

Phyllis Carver
Lakeland, FL

Croissants

1½ c. butter, softened
⅓ c. flour
¾ c. milk
¼ c. sugar
1 tsp. salt
2 pkg. dry yeast
½ c. 110 to 115-degree water
1 egg
3¾ to 4¼ c. flour
1 egg yolk
1 tbsp. milk

Cream butter and ⅓ cup flour in mixer bowl until light. Roll into 6x12-inch rectangle between waxed paper. Chill for 1 hour or longer. Heat ¾ cup milk, sugar and salt in saucepan until sugar is dissolved. Cool to lukewarm. Dissolve yeast in warm water. Combine cooled milk mixture, yeast and egg in bowl; mix well. Beat in 2 cups flour. Stir in as much remaining flour as possible with spoon. Knead on floured surface for 3 to 5 minutes or until smooth and elastic, kneading in enough remaining flour to make medium-soft dough. Let rest for 10 minutes. Roll into 14-inch square. Place chilled butter mixture on half the dough. Fold dough over to enclose butter; press edges to seal. Roll into 12x21-inch rectangle. Fold into thirds; seal edges. Chill, covered, in refrigerator. Repeat rolling, folding and chilling process 2 more times. Chill, covered, for several hours to overnight. Cut dough crosswise into 4 portions. Roll each portion into 12-inch circle. Cut each into 12 wedges. Roll each wedge loosely from wide end. Place point down on ungreased baking sheet; curve to form crescent. Let rise, covered, for 30 to 40 minutes or until doubled in bulk. Beat egg yolk with 1 tablespoon milk. Brush on rolls. Bake at 375 degrees for 12 to 15 minutes or until light brown. Yield: 48 rolls. Note: Prepared dough may be refrigerated for up to 1 week.

Delinda McCormick
Caldwell Co. H.S., Cadiz, KY

Special Sour Cream Rolls

2 pkg. dry yeast
½ c. warm water
1 c. sour cream
½ c. sugar
½ c. melted margarine
2 eggs, beaten
4 c. flour
1 tsp. salt
½ c. melted margarine

Dissolve yeast in warm water in large bowl. Blend sour cream and sugar with ½ cup melted margarine in small bowl. Stir into yeast mixture with eggs, flour and salt. Knead lightly on floured surface. Place in greased bowl, turning to grease surface. Let rise, covered, until doubled in bulk. Divide into 4 portions. Roll each portion into 12-inch circle on floured surface. Brush each with 2 tablespoons melted margarine. Cut each into 12 wedges; roll up from wide end. Shape into crescents on greased baking sheet. Let rise until doubled in bulk. Bake at 375 degrees for 10 to 12 minutes or until light brown. Yield: 48 rolls.

Jean Rapking
Harrison, WV

Hot Rolls For-A-Crowd

1½ c. dry yeast
8 c. warm water
6 c. sugar
½ c. salt
6 c. nonfat dry milk powder
4 c. eggs
3 c. oil
24 c. very warm water
23 lb. flour

Dissolve yeast in 8 cups warm water. Mix sugar, salt, milk powder, eggs, oil and 24 cups very warm water in large bowl. Stir in yeast mixture. Mix in flour gradually to make stiff dough. Knead on floured surface for 5 minutes. Place in very large oiled bowl; brush with oil. Let rise, covered, for 1½ hours or until doubled in bulk. Shape into balls. Arrange 8 rows of 12 rolls in 4 greased 17x25-inch baking pans. Let rise for 1½ hours or until doubled in bulk. Bake at 350 degrees for 25 minutes. Yield: 96 rolls per pan.

Bea Carlton
Nashville, TN

Refrigerator Rolls

2 pkg. dry yeast
¼ c. lukewarm water
2 eggs
2 c. milk, scalded, cooled
⅓ c. sugar
¼ c. melted butter
1 tbsp. salt
8 c. sifted flour

Dissolve yeast in lukewarm water. Beat eggs in mixer bowl. Add milk, sugar, butter, salt and yeast; mix well. Blend in 2 cups flour. Add 5 cups flour gradually, mixing well. Knead on surface sprinkled with remaining 1 cup flour until smooth and elastic. Place in greased bowl, turning to grease surface. Chill in refrigerator for 12 hours to 4 days. Punch dough down. Shape as desired. Place in greased baking pans. Let rise, covered, for 1 to 1½ hours or until doubled in bulk. Bake at 350 degrees for 30 minutes. Yield: 48 rolls.

Eula Mae Dyar
Puckett H.S., Mendenhall, MS

Pecan Rolls

1½ c. milk
½ c. sugar
4 tsp. salt
5 pkg. dry yeast
2 c. 105 to 115-degree water
6 eggs, beaten
15 to 16 c. sifted flour
1 c. butter
3 c. packed brown sugar
½ c. light corn syrup
3 c. broken pecans

Scald milk in saucepan. Add sugar, shortening and salt. Cool to lukewarm. Dissolve yeast in warm water in large bowl. Stir in milk mixture, eggs and half the flour. Add remaining flour; mix well. Knead on floured surface for 8 minutes or until smooth and elastic. Divide into 2 portions. Place in greased bowls, turning to grease surface. Let rise, covered, for 1½ to 2 hours or until doubled in bulk. Combine butter, brown sugar and corn syrup in saucepan. Heat until butter is melted. Stir in pecans. Spread evenly in 12 greased 8-inch baking pans. Punch dough down. Shape into balls. Place 6 balls in each pan. Let rise, covered, for 1 hour or until doubled in bulk. Bake at 350 degrees for 30 minutes. Invert immediately onto serving plates. Yield: 72 rolls.

Elsie S. Hilton
New Brockton Sch., New Brockton, AL

Easy Breadsticks

2 pkg. hot dog buns
4 sticks margarine, melted
2 tsp. garlic salt
2 tsp. oregano
2 to 4 tbsp. poppy seed
2 to 4 tbsp. sesame seed

Cut each bun lengthwise into 6 pieces. Dip into mixture of margarine, garlic salt and oregano to coat. Arrange close together on baking sheet. Sprinkle with mixture of poppy and sesame seed. Bake at 250 degrees for 1½ hours or until crisp. Cool. Store in airtight container. Yield: 96 breadsticks.

Lorraine Ireland
Providence, RI

Apple-Cinnamon Delights

2 tbsp. butter
½ c. packed brown sugar
¼ c. raisins
¼ c. red cinnamon candies
1 20-oz. can apple pie slices
¼ c. cinnamon candies
2 cans refrigerator cinnamon rolls
¼ c. raisins
½ c. chopped pecans

Melt butter at 200 degrees in electric skillet. Sprinkle brown sugar, ¼ cup raisins and ¼ cup cinnamon candies over butter. Add apple slices and remaining candies. Arrange rolls over top. Sprinkle with remaining raisins and pecans. Cook, covered, at 300 degrees for 20 to 25 minutes or until cooked through. Yield: 16 servings.

Ann McKnight
Charleston, SC

Butterscotch Buns

½ c. chopped nuts
2 10-oz. cans refrigerator biscuits
¼ c. melted margarine
½ c. sugar
1 tsp. cinnamon
1 6-oz. package butterscotch chips
⅓ c. evaporated milk

Sprinkle nuts into greased 9-inch cake pan. Separate biscuits. Dip into melted margarine; coat with mixture of sugar and cinnamon. Arrange overlapping biscuits in prepared pan. Bake at 400 degrees for 30 to 35 minutes or until light brown. Heat butterscotch chips and evaporated milk in saucepan until chips are melted. Pour over hot buns. Let stand for 5 minutes. Invert onto serving plate. Yield: 20 servings.

Polly Anne Bryant
Lonoke Jr. H.S., Lonoke, AR

Confetti Bread

1 c. each chopped green pepper, onion
1 c. butter
3 8-count cans refrigerator biscuits,
    cut into quarters
1 sm. jar bacon bits
½ c. Parmesan cheese

Sauté green pepper and onion in butter in skillet. Stir biscuits, bacon bits and cheese into vegetables. Spoon into greased bundt pan. Bake at 375 degrees for 30 minutes. Invert onto serving plate. Yield: 24 servings.

Sherrie Haub
Canton, OK

Cinnamon-Sugar Twists

2 cans flaky refrigerator biscuits
1 stick butter, melted
1 c. sugar
1 tsp. cinnamon
½ tsp. nutmeg
½ c. honey

Separate each biscuit into 2 thin biscuits. Pull each into strip and twist. Dip 1 side in butter then into mixture of sugar, cinnamon and nutmeg.

Place sugared side up on baking sheet. Bake at 425 degrees for 8 to 10 minutes or until brown. Mix remaining butter with honey. Brush over twists. Yield: 40 twists.

Kim Remington
Nowata, OK

Monkey Bread

½ c. sugar
½ tsp. cinnamon
3 cans refrigerator buttermilk biscuits
1 stick margarine
¾ c. sugar
¾ tsp. cinnamon

Mix ½ cup sugar and ½ teaspoon cinnamon in small bowl. Cut biscuits into quarters. Dip into cinnamon-sugar. Layer in greased and floured bundt pan. Melt margarine with remaining sugar and cinnamon in saucepan; stir until sugar dissolves. Pour over biscuits. Bake at 350 degrees for 30 to 35 minutes or until brown. Cool in pan for 5 minutes. Invert onto serving plate. Yield: 15 servings.

Lavern Frentzel
Perry Co. Sch., Uniontown, MD

Quick English Muffins

2 cans refrigerator buttermilk biscuits
Cornmeal

Separate biscuits. Flatten to size and shape of English muffins. Dredge in cornmeal. Heat greased skillet over medium heat. Arrange biscuits in hot skillet. Bake for 7 minutes on each side or until brown. Serve with jelly. Yield: 20 servings.

Peggy Matter
Naples, FL

DESSERTS

Apple Squares

2 egg yolks
1 tbsp. vinegar
3 c. flour
1 tsp. salt
1 c. shortening
Ice water
8 to 10 lg. apples
Lemon juice
2 to 3 c. sugar
2 tbsp. cornstarch
½ tsp. nutmeg
1 stick butter, sliced

Beat egg yolks with vinegar in small bowl. Combine flour and salt in bowl. Cut in shortening until crumbly. Add egg mixture and enough ice water to make sticky dough; handle as little as possible. Chill in refrigerator. Peel and slice apples. Toss with lemon juice in bowl. Mix sugar, cornstarch, cinnamon and nutmeg in bowl. Divide dough into 2 portions. Roll 1 portion to fit bottom and sides of 9 x 12-inch baking dish. Layer apples and sugar mixture ½ at a time in pastry-lined dish. Dot with butter. Top with remaining pastry; seal edges and cut vents. Sprinkle with additional sugar. Bake at 350 degrees for 1 hour and 15 minutes. Serve warm with vanilla ice cream. Store, covered, at room temperature. Yield: 20 servings.

Debra Greenwood
Clinton Jr. H.S., Knoxville, TN

Blueberry Crisp

2 c. flour
1 c. chopped pecans
3 sticks butter
3 c. confectioners' sugar
8 oz. cream cheese, softened
4 c. whipped topping
1 can blueberry pie filling

Mix flour and pecans in bowl. Cut in butter until crumbly. Pat into 9 x 13-inch baking dish. Bake at 275 degrees for 45 minutes. Cool. Cream confectioners' sugar and cream cheese in mixer bowl until light and fluffy. Fold in whipped topping. Spread over crust. Chill for 1 hour. Spread pie filling over top. Chill for 8 hours or longer. Cut into squares. Yield: 16 servings.

Karen R. Collins
Greensville Co. H.S., Emporia, VA

Award-Winning Cheesecake

2 c. graham cracker crumbs
½ c. confectioners' sugar
½ c. melted butter
1 c. sugar
16 oz. cream cheese, softened
4 eggs
2 tsp. lemon juice
2 cans cherry pie filling
2 c. whipped topping

Mix cracker crumbs, confectioners' sugar and melted butter in bowl until crumbly. Reserve ½ cup mixture. Press remaining crumbs over bottom of greased 9 x 13-inch baking dish. Cream sugar and cream cheese in mixer bowl until light and fluffy. Add eggs 1 at a time, mixing well after each addition. Spread in prepared pan. Bake at 350 degrees for 20 minutes. Cool. Mix lemon juice with pie filling in bowl. Spread over baked layer. Top with whipped topping and reserved crumbs. Chill overnight.
Yield: 12-15 servings.

Patricia M. Todd
Western Branch H.S., Suffolk, VA

Cheesecake

12 graham crackers, crushed
½ c. melted margarine
1   3-oz. package lemon gelatin
1 c. boiling water
1 c. sugar
8 oz. cream cheese, softened
1 tsp. vanilla extract
1   13-oz. can evaporated milk,
   well chilled

Mix graham cracker crumbs and margarine in bowl. Pat over bottom of 9 x 13-inch baking dish. Bake at 350 degrees for 10 minutes. Cool. Dissolve gelatin in boiling water in bowl or blender container. Add sugar, cream cheese and vanilla. Beat or blend until smooth. Whip evaporated milk in mixer bowl until soft mounds form. Blend in cream cheese mixture at low speed. Pour into prepared dish. Chill until serving time. Yield: 15 servings.

Barbara Tripp
Spring Lake Jr.-Sr. H.S., Springlake, MI

Prize Lemon Cheesecake

28 graham crackers, crushed
¼ c. sugar
½ tsp. cinnamon
¼ c. melted butter
16 oz. cream cheese, softened
1½ c. sugar
4 eggs, beaten
½ c. lemon juice
1 c. sour cream
¼ c. packed brown sugar
1 c. sour cream
2 tsp. lemon juice
1 tsp. grated lemon rind

Mix cracker crumbs, ¼ cup sugar, cinnamon and butter in bowl until crumbly. Press into two 9-inch pie plates. Beat cream cheese in mixer bowl until fluffy. Add 1½ cups sugar and eggs; beat until light. Stir in mixture of ½ cup lemon juice and 1 cup sour cream gradually. Pour into prepared pie plates. Bake at 350 degrees for 20 minutes. Combine remaining ingredients in bowl; mix well. Spread over cheesecake. Bake for 10 minutes longer. Cool on wire rack. Chill, covered, for 3 hours to 10 days. Yield: 16 servings.

Judy Meek
Marshall Jr. H.S., Wichita, KS

Miniature Cheesecakes

24 oz. cream cheese, softened
1 c. sugar
5 eggs
1½ tsp. vanilla extract
1 c. sour cream
¼ c. sugar
½ tsp. vanilla extract
Strawberry preserves

Beat cream cheese in bowl until smooth. Add 1 cup sugar gradually, beating until fluffy. Add eggs 1 at a time, mixing well after each addition. Stir in 1½ teaspoons vanilla. Fill paper-lined miniature muffin cups ⅔ full. Bake at 300 degrees for 30 minutes. Combine sour cream, ¼ cup sugar and ½ teaspoon vanilla in bowl; mix well. Spoon ¼ teaspoonful onto each cheesecake. Top with a small amount of strawberry preserves. Bake for 5 minutes longer. Yield: 72 servings.

Becki Fortner
Nashville, TN

Cherry Squares

1 c. butter, softened
2 c. sugar
4 eggs
½ tsp. vanilla extract
3 c. flour
½ tsp. baking powder
1   21-oz. can cherry pie filling
½ c. chopped pecans
¼ c. flour
¼ c. sugar
2 tbsp. margarine

Cream butter and 2 cups sugar in mixer bowl until light and fluffy. Add eggs; mix well. Mix in vanilla, 3 cups flour and baking powder. Spread half the mixture in greased 10x15-inch baking pan. Spread pie filling over dough. Spoon remaining dough over pie filling. Mix pecans and remaining ingredients in bowl until crumbly. Sprinkle over top. Bake at 350 degrees for 1 hour. Cut into squares. Yield: 16 servings.

Carla Seippel
Fort Osage Jr. H.S., Independence, MO

Dolly's Cherry Dessert

4½ c. flour
1 lb. margarine, melted
2 c. chopped nuts
4 c. confectioners sugar
16 oz. cream cheese, softened
Evaporated milk
12 to 15 c. vanilla pudding
2   No. 10 cans cherry pie filling
36 oz. whipped topping

Mix flour, margarine and nuts in bowl until crumbly. Press into 12x20-inch baking pan. Bake at 350 degrees until light brown. Cool. Cream confectioners' sugar and cream cheese in mixer bowl until light and fluffy. Add enough evaporated milk to make of spreading consistency. Spread evenly over crust. Layer pudding, pie filling and whipped topping over cream cheese mixture. Chill for 3 hours or longer. Yield: 50 servings.

Fonda Wren
Wichita H.S. West, Wichita, KS

Cherry Crumb Dessert

2   20-oz. cartons frozen cherries,
     thawed
½ tsp. almond extract
1 c. sifted flour
1 c. packed brown sugar
½ c. melted butter
1 tsp. allspice
½ tsp. nutmeg

Mix cherries and almond flavoring in 9x13-inch
baking dish. Combine remaining ingredients in
bowl; mix until crumbly. Sprinkle over cherries.
Bake at 325 degrees for 1 hour.
Yield: 12 servings.

Emma Ellen Bunyard
Jenks H.S., Jenks, OK

Cherry Delight

2½ c. graham cracker crumbs
¼ c. sugar
⅔ c. melted margarine
2 pkg. whipped topping mix
8 oz. cream cheese, softened
⅔ c. sugar
⅓ c. milk
2 cans cherry pie filling

Combine cracker crumbs, ¼ cup sugar and
margarine in bowl; mix until crumbly. Press into
9x13-inch baking dish. Bake at 350 degrees for
8 minutes. Cool. Prepare whipped topping
according to package directions. Beat cream
cheese, ⅔ cup sugar and milk in mixer bowl until
smooth. Fold in whipped topping. Spread over
crust. Spoon pie filling over top. Chill for 24
hours. Yield: 12 servings.

Ina H. Pack
Christiansburg H.S., Radford, VA

Aunt Madeline's Pink Frozen Dessert

1   20-oz. can cherry pie filling
1   20-oz. can crushed pineapple
1 lg. carton whipped topping
1 can sweetened condensed milk
1 c. chopped pecans

Combine pie filling, pineapple with juice,
whipped topping, condensed milk and ¾ cup

pecans in bowl; mix well. Spoon into 9x13-inch
pan. Sprinkle with remaining ¼ cup pecans.
Freeze until firm. Remove from freezer 2 to 3
hours before serving. Dessert should still contain
ice crystals when served. Yield: 16 servings.

Debi S. Corts
Stockbridge H.S., Stockbridge, MI

Cherry Dessert

1   16-oz. package graham crackers,
     crushed
1 c. melted margarine
2 c. sugar
16 oz. cream cheese, softened
16 oz. whipped topping
2   21-oz. cans cherry pie filling

Mix cracker crumbs and margarine in bowl.
Press mixture into two 9x13-inch baking dishes.
Bake at 325 degrees for 10 minutes. Cream
sugar and cream cheese in mixer bowl until light
and fluffy. Spread evenly over hot crusts. Cool.
Layer whipped topping and pie filling over cream
cheese mixture. Chill until serving time.
Yield: 32 servings.

Sharon Cooper
Chase H.S., Chase, KS

Cream Puffs

½ c. butter
1 c. water
¼ tsp. salt
1 c. flour
4 eggs

Bring butter, water and salt to a boil in saucepan.
Add flour all at once; stir vigorously until mixture
forms ball. Remove from heat. Add eggs 1 at a
time, beating well after each addition. Drop by
heaping spoonfuls onto well-greased baking
sheet. Bake at 450 degrees for 20 minutes.
Reduce temperature to 325 degrees. Bake for 20
minutes longer. Remove to wire rack to cool. Cut
off tops. Fill as desired. Puffs are excellent filled
with ice cream and topped with complementary
sauce. Yield: 12 servings.

Esther H. Nassar
Eric-Mason H.S., Toledo, OH

Dessert Pudding

¾ c. margarine, softened
1½ c. flour
1 c. crushed pecans
1 c. confectioners' sugar
8 oz. cream cheese, softened
12 oz. whipped topping
3   3-oz. packages chocolate instant
    pudding mix

Mix margarine, flour and pecans in bowl. Press into 9x13-inch baking dish. Bake at 350 degrees for 15 minutes. Cool. Cream confectioners' sugar and cream cheese in mixer bowl until light and fluffy. Blend in half the whipped topping. Spread evenly over baked layer. Prepare pudding mix according to package directions. Spread over cream cheese layer. Chill until set. Top with remaining whipped topping. Garnish with additional pecans or chocolate curls.
Yield: 12 servings.

Diane Zook
Larned H.S., Larned, KS

Four-Layer Delight

½ c. melted margarine
1 c. flour
1 c. chopped pecans
1 c. confectioners' sugar
8 oz. cream cheese, softened
1 c. whipped topping
2 sm. packages chocolate instant
    pudding mix
3 c. milk
9 oz. whipped topping

Mix margarine with flour and pecans in bowl. Press into 9x13-inch baking dish. Bake at 350 degrees for 15 minutes or until brown. Cool. Cream confectioners' sugar and cream cheese in mixer bowl until light and fluffy. Blend in 1 cup whipped topping. Spread over baked layer. Combine pudding mix and milk in bowl; mix until smooth. Spread over cream cheese layer. Top with remaining whipped topping and additional pecans. Chill until serving time.
Yield: 16 servings.

Gail Helms
Enterprise H.S., Enterprise, AL

Lemon Ice Cream

1½ c. lemon juice
4 c. sugar
1 c. whipping cream
6 c. milk
1 tbsp. grated lemon rind
Lemon twists

Blend lemon juice and sugar in bowl. Let stand for 30 minutes. Stir in remaining ingredients. Pour into 1-gallon ice cream freezer. Freeze according to manufacturer's instructions. Let ripen for 1½ to 2 hours. Spoon into serving dishes. Garnish with lemon twists.
Yield: 16-18 servings.

Sybil B. Murphy
Northwood H.S., Pittsboro, NC

Lemon Lust

1½ c. flour
1½ sticks margarine
¾ c. chopped pecans
1½ c. confectioners' sugar
9 oz. cream cheese, softened
1 lg. carton whipped topping
3   3-oz. packages lemon instant
    pudding mix
4 c. cold milk

Combine flour, margarine and pecans in bowl; mix until crumbly. Press into 9x13-inch baking dish. Bake at 375 degrees for 10 to 15 minutes or until brown; do not overbake. Cool. Cream confectioners' sugar and cream cheese in mixer bowl until light and fluffy. Blend in 1½ cups whipped topping. Spread over crust. Beat pudding mix and milk in bowl until thick. Spread over cream cheese layer. Top with remaining whipped topping. Chill until serving time.
Yield: 15 servings.

Betty K. Munsey
Bland H.S., Bland, VA

Peach Cobbler

4 c. sifted flour
2 tsp. salt
1⅓ c. shortening
½ c. ice water
2 tbsp. flour
¼ tsp. salt
1 c. sugar
1 tsp. almond extract
4 c. sliced peaches
½ stick butter, thinly sliced
2 tsp. cinnamon
Sugar

Mix 4 cups flour and 2 teaspoons salt in bowl. Cut in shortening until crumbly. Sprinkle ice water over flour mixture; mix gently just until mixture forms ball. Chill, wrapped in waxed paper, for several minutes. Roll into rectangle on floured surface; cut into 1-inch strips. Combine 2 tablespoons flour, ¼ teaspoon salt, 1 cup sugar and almond flavoring in bowl. Mix in peaches. Place half the peaches in buttered 9x11-inch baking dish. Dot with half the butter. Arrange strips over peaches, leaving small spaces between. Add layers of remaining peaches and strips in dish. Dot with butter between strips. Sprinkle with mixture of cinnamon and additional sugar. Bake at 350 degrees for 35 to 40 minutes or until brown. Yield: 12 servings.

Juanita Boyce
Lawton H.S., Lawton, OK

Pineapple Party Torte

1 2-layer pkg. yellow cake mix
1⅓ c. coconut
8 oz. cream cheese, softened
2 c. milk
1 sm. package vanilla instant pudding mix
1 20-oz. can crushed pineapple, drained
8 oz. whipped topping
1⅓ c. coconut

Prepare cake mix according to package directions, adding 1⅓ cups coconut. Pour into greased and floured 10x15-inch baking pan. Bake at 350 degrees for 20 minutes. Cool in pan for 10 minutes. Invert onto wire rack to cool completely. Invert carefully onto serving tray. Beat cream cheese in mixer bowl until fluffy. Add milk gradually, beating constantly. Add pudding mix. Beat at low speed for 2 minutes. Spread evenly over cake. Layer pineapple and whipped topping over pudding. Sprinkle with 1⅓ cups coconut. Chill until serving time. Yield: 15-20 servings.

Pat Foley
Tempe H.S., Tempe, AZ

Banana Pudding

1 6-oz. package pistachio instant pudding mix
3 c. milk
1 c. sour cream
16 oz. whipped topping
1 pkg. vanilla wafers
6 bananas, sliced

Combine pudding mix and milk in bowl; mix well. Let stand until thickened. Fold in sour cream and whipped topping. Layer vanilla wafers, bananas and pudding ⅓ at a time in 4-quart bowl. Garnish with vanilla wafer crumbs. Chill until serving time. Yield: 12 servings.

Wanda H. Ingle
Floyd Co. H.S., Floyd, VA

Bread Pudding

20 slices day-old bread
2 qt. milk, scalded
2 c. heavy cream
8 eggs
2 c. sugar
2 tsp. vanilla extract
2 tsp. cinnamon
1 tsp. nutmeg
½ c. melted butter
1 c. seedless raisins

Combine bread, milk and cream in large bowl. Beat eggs in bowl. Add sugar; mix well. Stir into bread mixture. Add remaining ingredients; mix well. Pour into 2 buttered 9x13-inch baking dishes. Place in larger pans with 1 inch hot water. Bake at 325 degrees for 1 hour or until knife inserted in center comes out clean. Serve with lemon sauce or boiled custard. Yield: 30 servings.

Kathy Thomas
Chickasha Mid. Sch., Chickasha, OK

Swedish Rice Pudding

1½ c. rice
2 c. water
1½ tsp. salt
9 c. milk
1 c. sugar
3 egg yolks
¼ c. milk
2 tsp. vanilla extract

Combine rice, water and salt in heavy 5-quart saucepan. Cook over high heat until water is absorbed. Add 2 cups milk. Reduce heat. Simmer for 15 to 20 minutes or until thickened, stirring constantly. Add 2 cups milk. Cook for 15 to 20 minutes, stirring constantly. Repeat process 2 more times adding 2 cups milk each time. Add 1 cup milk. Cook until thickened, stirring constantly. Mix in sugar. Beat egg yolks with ¼ cup milk in bowl. Stir 2 cups hot mixture into egg yolks; stir egg yolks into hot mixture. Cook for 3 minutes or just until thickened, stirring constantly. Stir in vanilla. Spoon into dessert bowls. Garnish with sprinkle of cinnamon. Yield: 12 servings.

Cindy Josephson
Johnson-Brock H.S., Johnson, NE

Vanilla Torte

½ c. margarine
1 c. flour
½ c. ground pecans
1 c. confectioners' sugar
8 oz. cream cheese, softened
8 oz. whipped topping
2 pkg. vanilla instant pudding mix
3 c. cold milk

Cut margarine into mixture of flour and pecans in bowl until crumbly. Press into 9x13-inch baking dish. Bake at 375 degrees for 15 minutes. Cool. Cream confectioners' sugar and cream cheese in mixer bowl until light and fluffy. Fold in 1 cup whipped topping. Spread in crust. Prepare pudding mix with milk according to package directions. Spread evenly over cream cheese layer. Top with remaining whipped topping. Chill until serving time. Yield: 12 servings.

Hazel Jolliffe
Rolling Meadows H.S., Arlington Heights, IL

Apricot-Filled Petits Fours

½ c. butter, softened
1¼ c. sugar
3 eggs
2 c. flour
1 tbsp. baking powder
½ tsp. salt
¾ c. milk
1 c. sugar
1 c. water
1 tbsp. apricot Brandy
Apricot preserves
Fondant Frosting

Cream butter and 1¼ cups sugar in bowl until light and fluffy. Add eggs 1 at a time, beating well after each addition. Add mixture of flour, baking powder and salt alternately with milk, mixing well after each addition. Pour into greased and floured 9x13-inch cake pan. Bake at 375 degrees for 25 minutes or until cake tests done. Cool for 10 minutes. Invert onto wire rack to cool completely. Wrap in foil; freeze for several hours. Split into 2 layers. Combine 1 cup sugar and water in saucepan. Simmer for 10 minutes. Remove from heat; add Brandy. Cool. Brush over layers. Spread preserves between layers. Cut into small squares. Place on wire rack in shallow pan. Pour warm Fondant Frosting over cakes, covering tops and sides. Let stand until icing is firm. Yield: 50 servings.

Fondant Frosting

6 c. sifted confectioners' sugar
5 tbsp. light corn syrup
1 tsp. vanilla extract
5 tbsp. water

Combine all ingredients in double boiler. Cook over boiling water until smooth and glossy. Tint as desired.

Photograph for this recipe on page 4.

Blackberry Wine Cake

1 pkg. white cake mix
1 c. blackberry wine
1   3-oz. package blueberrry gelatin
4 eggs, beaten
½ c. oil
⅓ c. blackberry wine
⅔ c. confectioners' sugar

Combine cake mix, 1 cup wine, gelatin, eggs and oil in mixer bowl. Beat until smooth. Pour into greased and floured bundt pan. Bake at 350 degrees for 40 minutes. Invert onto serving plate. Pierce cake with fork. Bring ⅓ cup wine to a boil in saucepan. Stir in confectioners' sugar. Pour over cake. Yield: 16 servings.

Sue Smith
Bartlesville H.S., Bartlesville, OK

Chocolate Sheet Cake

2 c. sugar
2 c. flour
1 tsp. cinnamon
½ tsp. salt
2 sticks margarine
3 tbsp. cocoa
1 c. water
2 eggs, beaten
½ c. buttermilk
1 tsp. soda
1 tsp. vanilla extract
1 stick margarine
3 tbsp. cocoa
6 tbsp. milk
16 oz. confectioners' sugar
1 tsp. vanilla extract
½ c. chopped nuts

Mix sugar, flour, cinnamon and salt in bowl. Combine 2 sticks margarine, 3 tablespoons cocoa and water in saucepan. Heat until margarine is melted; mix well. Pour over flour mixture; mix well. Combine eggs, buttermilk, soda and 1 teaspoon vanilla in bowl. Add to flour mixture; mix well. Pour into greased and floured 10x15-inch baking pan. Bake at 350 degrees for 20 minutes or until cake tests done. Heat 1 stick margarine, 3 tablespoons cocoa and milk in saucepan until margarine is melted. Pour over confectioners' sugar in bowl. Add vanilla; mix until smooth. Stir in nuts. Spread over warm cake. Yield: 16 servings.

Rebecca W. Harrell
Franklin-Simpson Mid. Sch., Franklin, KY

Hostess Giant Cupcake

2 pkg. dark chocolate cake mix
5 tbsp. flour
1 c. milk
1 c. sugar
½ c. shortening
½ c. butter, softened
½ tsp. salt
1 tsp. vanilla extract
½ c. butter
3 oz. unsweetened chocolate
3 c. confectioners' sugar
2¼ tsp. vanilla extract
3 to 6 tbsp. hot water

Prepare cake mixes according to package directions. Spoon into 2 greased and floured 9x13-inch baking pans. Bake according to package directions. Invert onto wire racks to cool. Combine flour and milk in saucepan. Cook until thickened, stirring constantly. Cool. Cream sugar, shortening, ½ cup butter, salt and 1 teaspoon vanilla in mixer bowl until light and fluffy. Add flour mixture; mix well. Spread over 1 cake. Top with remaining cake. Melt ½ cup butter in saucepan. Add chocolate; stir until melted. Stir in confectioners' sugar and 2¼ teaspoons vanilla. Add hot water 1 tablespoon at a time until glaze is of desired consistency. Drizzle over top and sides of cake.
Yield: 32 servings.

Sharon Cooper
Chase H.S., Chase, KS

Oatmeal Cake

    4 lb. butter, softened
    3 lb. shortening
    5 lb. sugar
    5 lb. brown sugar
    ½ c. vanilla extract
    1 tsp. lemon extract
    6 lb. flour
    1 lb. dried eggs
    1½ lb. dry milk powder
    2½ tbsp. soda
    6 tbsp. baking powder
    3 tbsp. salt
    4 tbsp. cinnamon
    2 tbsp. nutmeg
    5 lb. oats
    6 qt. water

Cream butter, shortening, sugars and flavorings in mixer bowl until light and fluffy. Sift flour, dried eggs, milk powder, soda, baking powder, salt and spices together. Add to creamed mixture alternately with oats and water, mixing well after each addition. Pour into 4 greased 16x24-inch baking pans and one 8x12-inch baking pan. Bake in 325-degree convection oven for 40 to 45 minutes or until cakes test done. Cool on wire rack. Spread with Topping. Cut into squares. Yield: 270 servings.

Topping

    ½ lb. butter, melted
    2½ lb. brown sugar
    1 c. flour
    6 lb. confectioners' sugar, sifted
    ¼ c. vanilla extract
    3 c. boiling water

Combine all ingredients in mixer bowl. Beat until smooth.

Onda Meyers
Northeastern H.S., Fountain City, IN

Pound Cake

    1 c. shortening
    2 c. sugar
    4 eggs
    ¼ tsp. soda
    1 c. buttermilk
    3 c. flour
    ¼ tsp. salt
    2 tbsp. vanilla extract
    2 tbsp. lemon extract
    1 tsp. almond extract
    ¼ c. melted butter
    1 c. confectioners' sugar
    ¼ c. lemon juice

Cream shortening and sugar in mixer bowl until light and fluffy. Add eggs 1 at a time, mixing well after each addition. Dissolve soda in buttermilk. Mix flour and salt. Add to creamed mixture alternately with buttermilk, mixing well after each addition. Stir in flavorings. Pour into greased and floured tube pan. Bake at 350 degrees for 1 hour or until cake tests done. Cool in pan on wire rack for 10 minutes. Invert onto serving plate. Combine remaining ingredients in bowl; mix well. Spoon over warm cake. Yield: 16 servings.

Lois Webber
East Forsyth H.S., Kernersville, NC

Six-Egg Pound Cake

    1 c. shortening
    3 c. sugar
    6 eggs
    2 tsp. vanilla extract
    1 tsp. butter extract
    1 tsp. lemon extract
    3 c. flour
    ¼ tsp. soda
    ½ tsp. salt
    1 c. buttermilk

Cream shortening and sugar in mixer bowl until light and fluffy. Add eggs and flavorings; mix well. Sift dry ingredients together. Add to cake batter alternately with buttermilk, mixing well after each addition. Pour into greased and floured bundt pan. Bake at 350 degrees for 1 hour. Cool in pan on wire rack for 10 minutes. Invert onto wire rack to cool completely. Yield: 16 servings.

Doretha C. Gilmore
Azalea Mid. Sch., Mobile, AL

Punch Bowl Cake

1 pkg. yellow cake mix
1 20-oz. can crushed pineapple
2 med. bananas, sliced
3 3-oz. packages vanilla instant
   pudding mix, prepared
1 qt. strawberries, sliced, sweetened
1 lg. carton whipped topping

Prepare and bake cake mix according to package directions for two 8-inch round cake pans. Cool on wire rack. Place 1 layer in punch bowl. Pierce with ice pick. Add layers of pineapple, bananas, half the pudding and remaining cake layer. Pierce cake with ice pick. Layer strawberries, remaining pudding and whipped topping over cake.
Yield: 20 to 25 servings.

Pat Vaughan
Fairfield Comm. H.S., Fairfield, IL

Orange Blossoms

2 pkg. yellow cake mix
Juice and grated rind of 4 oranges
Juice and grated rind of 4 lemons
3 lb. confectioners' sugar

Prepare cake mix according to package directions, reducing water by 4 teaspoons. Spoon into greased miniature muffin cups. Bake at 350 degrees for 10 minutes or until brown. Combine juices, rinds and confectioners' sugar in bowl; mix well. Dip cupcakes into sugar mixture; drain on wire rack.
Yield: 150 miniature cupcakes.

Vivian Pike
Bunker Hill H.S., Claremont, NC

Monster Cookies

1 lb. margarine, softened
2 lb. brown sugar
4 c. sugar
1 tbsp. light corn syrup
3 lb. crunchy peanut butter
12 eggs
8 tsp. soda
1 tbsp. vanilla extract
18 c. quick-cooking oats
1 lb. chocolate chips
1 lb. M and M's chocolate candies

Combine margarine, brown sugar, sugar, corn syrup, peanut butter, eggs, soda and vanilla in mixer bowl; mix well. Mix remaining ingredients in bowl. Stir into cookie batter. Drop by tablespoonfuls onto cookie sheet. Bake at 350 degrees for 12 minutes or just until brown. Remove to wire rack to cool.
Yield: 10-20 dozen.

Teresa Mcquire
Fairfield Comm. H.S., Fairfield, IL
Mary Alice Lee
Kaukauwa H.S., Hilbert, WI
Judy Meek
Marshall Jr. H.S., Wichita, KS

Peanut Butter Bars

4 lb. butter, softened
1 gal. peanut butter
10½ lb. sugar
1 c. vanilla extract
1 tsp. lemon extract
6 lb. flour, sifted
2½ lb. dried eggs
9 c. water
4 c. chocolate chips

Cream butter, peanut butter, sugar and flavorings in mixer until light. Add flour and dried eggs alternately with water, mixing well after each addition. Mix in chocolate chips. Pour into 4 lightly greased 16x24-inch baking pans and one 8x12-inch baking pan. Bake in convection oven at 325 degrees for 30 to 40 minutes or until bars test done. Cool on wire rack. Drizzle with Icing. Cut into bars. Yield: 25 dozen.

Icing

2½ c. sugar
¾ c. cocoa
1½ c. dried milk powder
1½ lb. butter
1½ c. water
¼ c. vanilla extract
4 lb. confectioners' sugar, sifted

Combine sugar, cocoa and milk powder in large mixer bowl. Bring butter, water and vanilla to a boil in saucepan. Add to cocoa mixture; mix well. Add confectioners' sugar; beat until smooth.

Onda Meyers
Northeastern H.S., Fountain City, IN

Brownies For-A-Crowd

8 eggs, beaten
4½ c. sugar
2 c. flour
1 tsp. vanilla extract
½ lb. chocolate, melted
1 lb. butter, melted
1½ lb. chopped nuts

Combine eggs, sugar and flour in bowl; mix well. Stir in remaining ingredients. Spread ¾ inch thick in 2 greased 10x15-inch baking pans. Bake at 350 degrees for 40 minutes; do not overbake. Cut into 2x3-inch pieces. Remove immediately to wire rack to cool. Yield: 50 brownies.

Lenorah Polk
Edmond, OK

Old-Fashioned Orange Icebox Cookies

1 c. butter, softened
½ c. sugar
½ c. packed light brown sugar
1 egg
2 tbsp. orange juice
⅛ tsp. vanilla extract
2½ c. flour
¼ tsp. each soda, salt
1 tbsp. grated orange rind
½ c. chopped pecans

Cream butter and sugars in bowl until light. Beat in egg, orange juice and vanilla. Sift in flour, soda and salt; mix well. Stir in orange rind and pecans. Chill for several minutes. Shape into two 1¼-inch diameter rolls; wrap in waxed paper. Chill for 3 hours or until firm. Cut into ³⁄₁₆-inch slices. Place ½ inch apart on ungreased cookie sheet. Bake at 375 degrees for 8 or 9 minutes or until light brown. Do not overbake. Remove to wire rack to cool. Yield: 11 dozen.

Doris Boggs
Harrison, WV

Dishpan Cookies

2 c. packed brown sugar
2 c. sugar
2 c. oil
4 eggs
1 tbsp. soda
½ tsp. baking powder

1 tsp. salt
4 c. flour
1½ c. oatmeal
2 c. flaked coconut
4 c. cornflakes
1   6-oz. package chocolate chips
1   6-oz. package butterscotch chips

Combine all ingredients in order given in very large bowl; mix well. Drop by spoonfuls onto cookie sheet. Bake at 325 degrees for 10 to 12 minutes. Yield: 14 dozen.

Glenda Nemecek
Purcell, OK

Fruitcake Bars

2 c. packed brown sugar
2½ c. water
⅔ c. shortening
4 c. raisins
4 c. flour
2 tsp. salt
2 tsp. each baking powder, soda
1 tsp. each nutmeg, cloves
4 tsp. cinnamon
1 c. chopped nuts
Confectioners' sugar

Bring first 4 ingredients to a boil in saucepan. Cool. Combine dry ingredients in bowl. Add cooled mixture and nuts; mix well. Press into 2 greased 9x13-inch baking pans. Bake at 350 degrees for 35 to 40 minutes or until light touch leaves no imprint. Cool. Sprinkle with confectioners' sugar. Cut into bars. Yield: 6 dozen.

Celeste Warley
Cleveland, OH

South Garland Pie Crusts

10 c. flour
3 tbsp. salt
4½ c. shortening
1½ c. plus 2 tbsp. cold water

Combine flour and salt in bowl. Mix in shortening with hands until crumbly. Add water; mix well. Divide into 12 portions. Store, wrapped in plastic wrap, in freezer. Yield: 12 pie shells.

Marcia Ingram
Lexington H.S., Lexington, TX

Deep-Dish Blueberry Pies

1½ c. sugar
6 tbsp. Argo cornstarch
12 c. blueberries
2 tsp. grated lemon rind
1 recipe 2-crust pie pastry

Mix sugar and cornstarch in bowl. Add blueberries and lemon rind; toss to coat well. Spoon into 2 deep-dish pie plates. Top with pastry. Flute edges; cut vents. Bake at 425 degrees for 30 to 35 minutes or until brown. Yield: 14 servings.

Photograph for this recipe on Cover.

Lemon Chiffon Velvet Pies

2 env. unflavored gelatin
½ c. cold water
6 eggs, separated
1 c. sugar
1 c. fresh lemon juice
1 tsp. salt
1 tbsp. grated lemon rind
1 c. sugar
1 c. whipping cream, whipped
2 baked 9-in. pie shells

Soften gelatin in cold water. Combine beaten egg yolks, 1 cup sugar, lemon juice and salt in double boiler. Cook over boiling water for 10 minutes or until thickened, stirring constantly. Remove from heat. Stir in gelatin mixture and lemon rind. Chill until slightly thickened. Beat egg whites in bowl until soft peaks form. Fold in gelatin mixture and stiffly whipped cream gently. Spoon into pie shells. Chill until set. Garnish with additional whipped cream. Yield: 12-16 servings.

Judy Meek
Marshall Jr. H.S., Wichita, KS

Frosty Mint Ice Cream Pies

1 pkg. chocolate mint
or devil's food cake mix
1 can prepared fudge frosting
¾ c. water
¼ c. oil
1½ qt. mint-chocolate chip ice
cream, softened

Combine cake mix, ¾ cup frosting, water and oil in mixer bowl; beat at low speed until moistened. Beat at high speed for 2 minutes. Spread evenly over botton of 2 greased 9-inch pie plates. Bake at 350 degrees for 25 to 30 minutes. Do not overbake; mixture will rise and then fall to form pie shells. Cool completely. Spread ice cream in shells. Heat remaining frosting in saucepan just until softened. Drop by spoonfuls onto ice cream; swirl with knife. Freeze for 2 hours or longer. Yield: 12-16 servings.

Cynthia Kolberg
Fairfield Jr.-Sr. H.S., Goshen, IN

Ginger Peachy Lattice Pies

6 tbsp. Argo cornstarch
1½ c. sugar
12 c. sliced peeled peaches
2 tbsp. lemon juice
2 tsp. grated fresh ginger
2 recipes 2-crust pie pastry

Mix cornstarch and sugar in bowl. Add peaches, lemon juice and ginger; toss to coat well. Spoon into 2 pastry-lined pie plates. Roll remaining pastry into two 12-inch circles. Cut each into ten ½-inch strips. Weave strips into lattice top. Seal edges and flute. Sprinkle with additional sugar. Bake at 425 degrees for 40 to 50 minutes or until brown. Yield: 14 servings.

Photograph for this recipe on Cover.

Tropical Pineapple-Strawberry Pies

2 c. sugar
½ c. Argo cornstarch
4 c. cubed fresh pineapple
6 c. sliced strawberries
¼ c. rum
2 unbaked 9-in. pie shells
1 c. flour
⅔ c. sugar
½ c. coconut
⅔ c. margarine

Mix 2 cups sugar and cornstarch in bowl. Add pineapple, strawberries and rum; toss to coat well. Spoon into pie shells. Mix flour, ⅔ cup sugar and coconut in bowl. Cut in margarine until crumbly. Sprinkle over pies. Bake at 425 degrees for 15 minutes. Reduce temperature to 350 degrees. Bake for 30 minutes longer. Yield: 14 servings.

Photograph for this recipe on Cover.

QUANTITIES TO SERVE 50

Food	For 50 Servings	Size of Each Serving
BEVERAGES		
Carbonated beverages	25 16-ounce bottles	1 cup
Cocoa, for hot chocolate	3 cups	1 cup
Coffee, ground	1½ pounds	1 cup
Coffee, instant	6 ounces	¾ cup
Cream, for coffee	1¼ quarts	1½ tablespoons
Fruit juice concentrates, frozen	54 ounces	½ cup
Fruit or tomato juice, canned	4 46-ounce cans	½ cup
Lemon, for tea	5 large	1 slice
Lemonade concentrate, frozen	78 ounces	1 cup
Punch	2 gallons	⅔ cup
Sugar, lump	1⅛ pounds	2 lumps
Tea, bulk	4 ounces	¾ cup
Tea, instant	1¼ ounces	1 cup
DAIRY		
Butter	1¾ pounds	1 tablespoon
Cheese, to shred	6 pounds	2 tablespoons
Cream, to whip	1 quart	1 tablespoon
Ice cream	2 gallons	1 large scoop
Milk	3 gallons	1 cup
MEAT, POULTRY, FISH		
Bacon	6 pounds	2 slices
Beef, boneless roast	25 pounds	8 ounces
Beef, rib roast	35 pounds	12 ounces
Chicken salad	6¼ quarts	½ cup
Chicken, to roast	35-40 pounds	6 ounces
Chicken, for dishes using chopped cooked chicken	20-25 pounds	
Fish fillets	13 pounds	4 ounces
Ground beef, for patties	12½-15 pounds	4-5 ounces
Ground beef, for meat loaf	12 pounds	4 ounces
Ham, bone in, to bake	22-25 pounds	5-6 ounces
Ham, canned	14 pounds	4 ounces
Lamb, leg to roast	25 pounds	8 ounces

Quantities To Serve 50

Food	For 50 Servings	Size of Each Serving
MEAT, POULTRY, FISH		
Oysters, for stew	6 quarts	2 cups stew
Oysters, to scallop	6 quarts	½ cup
Pork chops	17 pounds (3/lb.)	5-6 ounces
Pork, loin to roast	25 pounds	8 ounces
Salmon, for salad	8 16-oz. cans	½ cup
Sausage	12½ pounds	4 ounces
Shrimp, in shell	20 pounds	4 ounces
Shrimp, peeled	12 pounds	4 ounces
Tuna, for salad	16 cans	½ cup
Turkey, to roast	35-40 pounds	8 ounces
Turkey, for dishes using chopped cooked turkey	16 pounds	
Wieners	12 pounds	4 ounces
SALADS AND RELISHES		
Apples, for sauce	25 pounds	½ cup
Cabbage, for slaw	12-15 pounds	5-6 ounces
Carrots, strips	6¼ pounds	2 ounces
Celery, strips	6¼ pounds	2 ounces
Cranberry sauce	6 pounds	½-inch slice
Fruit cocktail	12 16-ounce cans	4 ounces
Fruit salad	9 quarts	¾ cup
Fruits, canned	7 29-ounce cans	4 ounces
Lettuce	12 medium heads	¼ head
Lettuce leaves	6 heads	2-3 leaves
Mayonnaise	1 quart	1⅓ tablespoons
Nuts	3¼ pounds	1 ounce
Pickles	2½ quarts	1 ounce
Potato salad	6½ quarts	½ cup
Salad dressing	1-1½ quarts	2 tablespoons
Tomatoes	30 medium	3 slices
Vegetable salad	10 quarts	¾ cup

Quantities To Serve 50

Food	For 50 Servings	Size of Each Serving
SANDWICHES		
Beef, roast, sliced	5 pounds	1 slice
Bread, sandwich	6 pounds	2 slices
Cheese, sliced	3¼ pounds	1 slice
Ham, baked, sliced	5 pounds	1 slice
Jam or preserves	1½ quarts	1 sandwich
Peanut Butter	1½ quarts	1 sandwich
VEGETABLES		
Asparagus, canned	14 pounds	4-6 spears
Asparagus, fresh	20 pounds	4-5 spears
Beans, dried	4½ pounds	3 ounces
Cabbage	7 heads	⅛ head
Canned vegetables	14 pounds	½ cup
Carrots	13 pounds	4 ounces
Cauliflowerets	13 pounds	4 ounces
Corn on cob	50 ears	1 ear
Frozen vegetables	16 10-oz. packages	½ cup
Green beans, fresh	12½ pounds	4 ounces
Onions, to cream	15 pounds	½ cup
Potatoes, to mash or scallop	15 pounds	½ cup
Potatoes, frozen French-fried	13 pounds	4 ounces
Sweet potatoes	25 pounds	8 ounces
MISCELLANEOUS		
Cake mix	3-4 packages	1 slice
Crackers	1 pound	2 crackers
Gelatin	13 3-oz. packages	½ cup
Ice, for tea	50 pounds	
Macaroni	4½ pounds	¾ cup
Minute rice	6 15-oz. packages	¾ cup
Noodles	48 ounces	½ cup
Potato chips	3 pounds	1 ounce
Pudding	12 4-oz. packages	½ cup
Rolls	6½ dozen	1½ rolls
Soup, canned	20 cans	1 cup
Spaghetti	4½ pounds	¾ cup

INDEX
All microwave recipe pages are preceded by an M.

COOKBOOK ORDER FORM

BOOK TITLE	Item#	Qty.	Price	Total
			Subtotal	
			Add state & local tax	
			Total Payment	

mm

**To place your charge card orders,
call our toll-free number
1-800-251-1542
or clip and mail convenient order form.**

Name _____

Address _____

City _____ State _____ Zip _____

Daytime Phone   (____) _____

☐   Payment enclosed.

☐   Please Charge My: ☐ MasterCard   ☐ Visa

Expiration Date _____

Account Number _____

Signature _____

- No COD orders please.
- Prices subject to change
  without notice.
- Books offered subject
  to availability.
- Make checks payable to
  Great American Opportunities.

**Please mail completed
order form to:**

**Great American Opportunities,
Inc.
P. O. Box 77, Nashville, TN 37202**